RECENT PROGRESS IN PARALLEL AND DISTRIBUTED COMPUTING

Edited by **Wen-Jyi Hwang**

Recent Progress in Parallel and Distributed Computing
http://dx.doi.org/10.5772/65177
Edited by Wen-Jyi Hwang

Contributors

Wen-Jyi Hwang, Tong Ming Lim, Hock Yeow Yap, Alex Papalexopoulos, Ignacio Aravena, Anthony Papavasiliou, Abdelrahman Osman, Vaidas Giedrimas, Leonidas Sakalauskas, Anatoly Petrenko, Wolfgang Ossadnik, Ralf H. Kaspar, Benjamin Föcke

Published by InTech

Janeza Trdine 9, 51000 Rijeka, Croatia

Notice

Statements and opinions expressed in the chapters are these of the individual contributors and not necessarily those of the editors or publisher. No responsibility is accepted for the accuracy of information contained in the published chapters. The publisher assumes no responsibility for any damage or injury to persons or property arising out of the use of any materials, instructions, methods or ideas contained in the book.

Publishing Process Manager Nina Kalinic
Technical Editor SPi Global
Cover InTech Design team

First published July, 2017
Printed in Croatia
Legal deposit, Croatia: National and University Library in Zagreb

Additional hard copies can be obtained from orders@intechopen.com

Recent Progress in Parallel and Distributed Computing, Edited by Wen-Jyi Hwang
p. cm.
Print ISBN 978-953-51-3315-5
Online ISBN 978-953-51-3316-2

For EU product safety concerns:
IN TECH d.o.o., Prolaz Marije Krucifikse Kozulić 3, 51000 Rijeka, Croatia,
info@intechopen.com or visit our website at intechopen.com.

Meet the editor

Wen-Jyi Hwang received the MSECE and PhD degrees from the University of Massachusetts Amherst, Amherst, MA, USA, in 1990 and 1993, respectively. From September 1993 to January 2003, he was with the Department of Electrical Engineering, Chung Yuan Christian University, Taiwan. In February 2003, he joined the Department of Computer Science and Information Engineering, National Taiwan Normal University, Taipei, Taiwan, where he is currently a full professor. From 2006 to 2010, he also served as the chairman of the same department. His research interests include parallel computing systems, Internet of things, reconfigurable computing, field-programmable gate array fast prototyping, and system on chip. Dr. Hwang is the recipient of the 2002 Outstanding Young Researcher Award from the Asia-Pacific Board of the IEEE Communication Society and 2002 Outstanding Young Electrical Engineer Award from the Chinese Institute of the Electrical Engineering.

Contents

Preface

The parallel and distributed computing is an exciting paradigm that provides computing and communication services for data and/or computation-intensive applications. Large varieties of devices and systems can be accessed for effective parallel and distributed computing. We can easily use general purpose graphic processing unit (GPU) for high-speed computation. Cluster or cloud technologies and systems are the effective alternatives. Embedded systems and Internet of things technology may also be beneficial for the implementation of distributed systems. The proliferation of parallel and distributed systems further spurs the demand for data-intensive and/or computation-intensive applications. This emergence is an outcome of research and technological advances in computer architectures, software, and network.

In this book, chapters that would capture cutting-edge research activity in new parallel and distributed computing technologies are solicited. These chapters introduce new studies in the fields of computer applications, architectures, software, and network for parallel and distributed computing. We believe that all of these chapters are of very high quality and can also stimulate future research innovations in this area.

This book is organized as follows. The first chapter provides an overview of this book. Chapters 2 and 3 present new algorithms and models for the applications of social network and grid computing, respectively. The studies on GPU are discussed in Chapter 4. The final two chapters focus on the software implementation and evaluation.

I would like to thank all recruited authors for their scholarly contributions. I am also grateful to InTech staff for publishing this book and especially to Ms. Nina Kalinic, for her kind assistance throughout the editing process. Without them, this book would not be possible. Finally, on behalf of all the authors, I hope that the readers will benefit in many ways from reading this book.

Wen-Jyi Hwang
Department of Computer Science and Information Engineering
National Taiwan Normal University
Taipei, Taiwan

Chapter 1

Introductory Chapter: The Newest Research in Parallel and Distributed Computing

Wen-Jyi Hwang

Additional information is available at the end of the chapter

http://dx.doi.org/10.5772/intechopen.69201

The parallel and distributed computing is concerned with concurrent use of multiple compute resources to enhance the performance of a distributed and/or computationally intensive application. The compute resources may be a single computer or a number of computers connected by a network. A computer in the system may contain single-core, multi-core and/or many-core processors. The design and implementation of a parallel and distributed system may involve the development, utilization and integration of techniques in computer network, software and hardware. With the advent of networking and computer technology, parallel and distributed computing systems have been widely employed for solving problems in engineering, management, natural sciences and social sciences.

There are six chapters in this book. From Chapters 2 to 6, a wide range of studies in new applications, algorithms, architectures, networks, software implementations and evaluations of this growing field are covered. These studies may be useful to scientists and engineers from various fields of specialization who need the techniques of distributed and parallel computing in their work.

The second chapter of this book considers the applications of distributed computing for social networks. The chapter entitled "A Study on the Node Influential Capability in Social Networks by Incorporating Trust Metrics" by Tong-Ming Lim and Hock Yeow Yap provides useful distributed computing models for the evaluation of node influential capacity in social networks. Two algorithms are presented in this study: Trust-enabled Generic Algorithm Diffusion Model (T-GADM) and Domain-Specified Trust-enabled Generic Algorithm Diffusion Model (DST-GADM). Experimental results confirm the hypothesis that social trust plays an important role in influential propagation. Moreover, it is able to increase the rate of success in influencing other social nodes in a social network.

Another application presented in this book is the smart grid for power engineering. The chapter entitled "A Distributed Computing Architecture for the Large-Scale Integration of

Renewable Energy and Distributed Resources in Smart Grids" by Ignacio Aravena, Anthony Papavasiliou and Alex Papalexopoulos analyzes the distributed system for the management of the short-term operations of power systems. They propose optimization algorithms for both the levels of the distribution grid and high voltage grids. Numerical results are also included for illustrating the effectiveness of the algorithms.

This book also contains a chapter covering the programming aspect of parallel and distributed computing. For the study of parallel programming, the general processing units (GPUs) are considered. GPUs have received attention for parallel computing because their many-core capability offers a significant speedup over traditional general purpose processors. In the chapter entitled "GPU Computing Taxonomy" by Abdelrahman Ahmed Mohamed Osman, a new classification mechanism is proposed to facilitate the employment of GPU for solving the single program multiple data problems. Based on the number of hosts and the number of devices, the GPU computing can be separated into four classes. Examples are included to illustrate the features of each class. Efficient coding techniques are also provided.

The final two chapters focus on the software aspects of the distributed and parallel computing. Software tools for the wikinomics-oriented development of scientific applications are presented in the chapter entitled "Distributed Software Development Tools for Distributed Scientific Applications" by Vaidas Giedrimas, Anatoly Petrenko and Leonidas Sakalauskas. The applications are based on service-oriented architectures. Flexibilities are provided so that codes and components deployed can be reused and transformed into a service. Some prototypes are given to demonstrate the effectiveness of the proposed tools.

The chapter entitled "DANP-Evaluation of AHP-DSS" by Wolfgang Ossadnik, Benjamin Föcke and Ralf H. Kaspar evaluates the Analytic Hierarchy Process (AHP)-supporting software for the use of adequate Decision Support Systems (DSS) for the management science. The corresponding software selection, evaluation criteria, evaluation framework, assessments and evaluation results are provided in detail. Issues concerning the evaluation assisted by parallel and distributed computing are also addressed.

These chapters offer comprehensive coverage of parallel and distributed computing from engineering and science perspectives. They may be helpful to further stimulate and promote the research and development in this rapid growing area. It is also hoped that newcomers or researchers from other areas of disciplines desiring to learn more about the parallel and distributed computing will find this book useful.

Author details

Wen-Jyi Hwang

Address all correspondence to: whwang@csie.ntnu.edu.tw

Department of Computer Science and Information Engineering, National Taiwan Normal University, Taipei, Taiwan

Chapter 2

Social Trust: Evaluating Node Influential Capability in Social Networks

Yap Hock Yeow and Lim Tong-Ming

Additional information is available at the end of the chapter

http://dx.doi.org/10.5772/67021

Abstract

Social networking sites are platforms that facilitate large-scale information sharing activities in recent years. Many organizations analyze social networking traffic to gain market insights in order to observe the latest market trends. These analyses also allow organizations to identify key promoters who have strong influences on these social networking platforms to promote their products or services. It is hypothesized that social trust plays an important role in influential propagation, and it is able to increase the rate of success in influencing other social nodes in a social network. This research performs large-scale experimental simulation to study the influential outcome with and without the presence of social trust in the social nodes.

Keywords: influence diffusion, influential maximization, social trust, trusted influence, domain specified trust influence

1. Introduction

In the last decade, the number of social networking site users have increased leap and bound [1]. Social networking sites are great places for one to express opinions toward people, products or services. Social networking sites disseminate information by influencing current and new nodes within the social networking environment. Gesenhues [2], Paquette [3] and Quesenberry [4] found that recommendations on the social networking sites often highly regarded by consumers. A research carried out by Ewing [5] showed that consumers often rely extensively on social networking sites referrals to make consumer decisions. In a world with many uncertainties, interacting with anonymous often raises trust issue. Trust presented various concerns especially for business operators where information spreading on the social networking sites may alter reputational impacts toward a business. There are many trust-related studies [6–9] that were conducted by different researchers, and most of them strongly supported that trust played a key role in affecting one's decision. Without doubt, the use of social networking sites for large-scale information sharing and message spreading is effective [10–12], but there are still some shortcomings that need to be addressed where it includes online user-generated contents and the assessment on their credibility. This research suggests two approaches to investigate trust as a factor on influential maximization and trust with domain specified social nodes as a factor on influential maximization. The objective of this research is to uncover trust value of each social node by evaluating social node opinion consistency and then to evaluate the rate of successful influenced social nodes with and without the presence of trust and domain specified trust. This research formulates two hypothesizes. They are as follows: (1) trust is able to positively increase the rate of successfully influenced social nodes within a social networking site, and (2) trust is able to positively increase the rate of successfully influenced social nodes from trusted social networking site users that are in the same domain. This research also reviewed extensively on trust and trust-related implementation issues on social networking sites. This article will report the results gathered from the findings and presents a discussion of the two hypothesizes with a conclusion.

2. Related works

Constant engagement on social networking sites significantly raises the chance of exposing one's identity either voluntarily or not voluntarily [13]. Excessive disclosure of one's personal information raises privacy-related issue and threat. In order to minimize the risk of overexposure one's identity, most if not all users on social networking sites [14] masked themselves using an Internet Identity (IID). They use IID to disguise themselves while communicating with others on these social networking sites. The process of uncovering the true identity of an online user one interacts with may not be easy as people constantly adopting new strategies to restrict the amount of information being disclosed on these social networking sites. Social networking sites play an important role at spreading information, news or ideas to all the connected nodes. Social networking sites create an endless source of information that is readily available for its users, but it is also undeniably that not all information obtained from social networking sites is always accurate and reliable. The fact that many social networking site readers and consumers rely extensively on the information obtained from these social networking sites to make their decision worried many business operators. Information spreading around social networking sites can change the public's viewpoint toward a product or service. Most of the user-generated contents on social networking sites are text, it is always important for business operators to extract and analyze these user-generated contents to identify key promoters and detractors and, at the same time, to identify genuine and trustable contents. **Figure 1** illustrates how an opinion flows from different sources and how information is perceived at the recipients.

Given the innumerable amount of information easily obtainable online, trusting a piece of information has always been a concern. In order to trust any content, it is important to understand what trust is. Trust is the most fundamental motivation behind different people cooperating together toward a common goal. There is no absolute definition of how trust can

http://dx.doi.org/10.5772/67021

be initiated because the definition of trust varies for different applications, and it is always situational specific. Different researchers and research areas may also have their own definition of trust such as,

- Trust is defined as willingness to rely on the other partner of the relationship [15].
- Trust is the expectation of belief that any opportunistic behavior will appear by others [16].
- Trust of one's performance depends on the actions of the counterpart [17].
- Trust increases when expectations of the other party are consistently and reliably met, and decreases when the other party acts otherwise [18].
- Trust is a mentality action a person uses while trying to reduce uncertainty and complexity when reaching an agreement [19].
- Trust is the subjective probability by which an individual, A, expects that another individual, B, performs a given action on which its welfare depends [20].
    - Challenged: Falcone & Castelfranchi—having high reliability in a person in general does not necessarily sufficient to decide such person is very dependable [21].

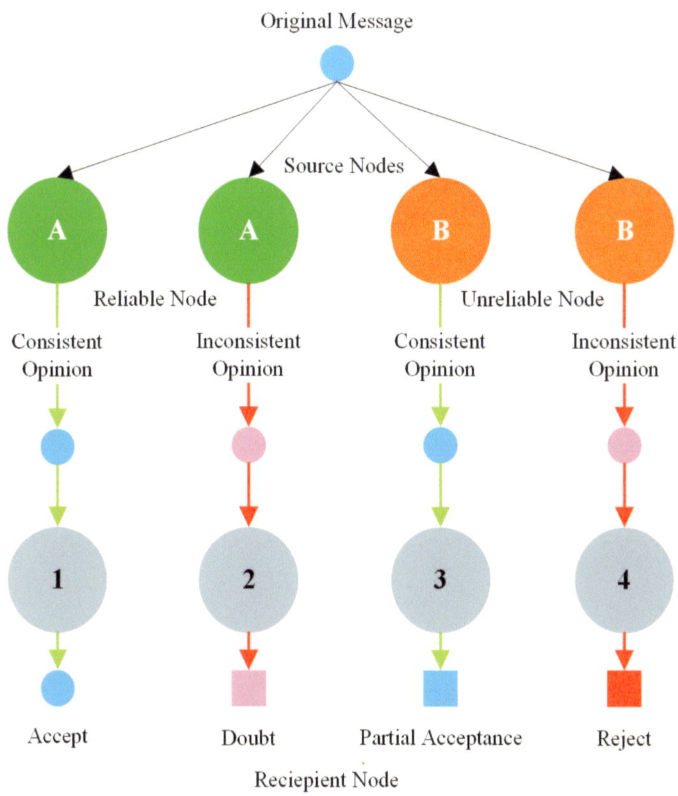

Figure 1. Opinion propagation model.

It is also said that the value of trust changes when it is being applied differently. The Trust Referent Characteristic table developed by Mcknight [22] best describes the trust-related characteristics that a node may display in an online environment. In this research, the Trust Referent Characteristics table has been improved with additional identified values by analyzing datasets obtained from [23–25]. **Table 1** shows the updated Trust Referent Characteristic table.

This research examines the integrity of user-generated contents (highlighted in grey) as a form of trust on the social networking sites. Since social networking sites contain large amount of unstructured texts, content integrity can be analyzed by adopting text analysis algorithms from many researchers [26–29]. Algorithmic details and latest research application updates can be found in Ref. [30, 31]; therefore, it will not be covered in this article. Diffusion equations used in this research are formulated using Kempe's [32, 33] activation function. Eq. (1) illustrates Kempe's function:

$$P_v(u,S) = \frac{f_v(S \cup \{u\}) - f_v(S)}{1 - f_v(S)} \quad (1)$$

Trust-related characteristic	Second-order conceptual category
Competent	
Expert	
Experience	
Dynamic	Competence
Predictable	
Foresight	Predictability
Good moral	
Good will	
Benevolent, Caring	
Responsive	Benevolence
Honest	Integrity
Credible	
Reliable Dependable	
Openness	
Careful	Psychology, mentality
Shared understanding	
Contemplation	Knowledgeable
Personally attractive	Prospect

Table 1. Trust referent characteristic table.

http://dx.doi.org/10.5772/67021

3. Research methodology

The process of profiling trust involves two stages where the first stage uses Texted Oriented Opinion Mining [30] algorithm to analyze user-generated text contents of each social node and return a trust probability score with a minimum value of 0 and a maximum value of 1, and the second stage is to analyze the cumulative objective score of each social node's text contents. The simulation uses Matlab r2016a in the experiment where genetic algorithm diffusion model (GADM) is the base algorithm that performs the influential diffusion. The Virtual Social Node (VSN) algorithm plays a simple yet important role in the influential diffusion process by simulating a virtual social network consisting of nodes and relationship links between nodes. The virtual social network simulated by VSN is structured as $a \cup b$ or $c \cap (a \cup b)$ (**Figure 2**) such that A is the highest superset of all nodes in the social network, and $a, b, c \ldots n$ are subsets of A denoted as $\{a, b, c \ldots n\} \subset A$ and consist of a total of 5117944 social nodes. The influence diffusion adopts the bottom-up approach where it initiates from the lowest subset all the way to the highest superset. These algorithms had been published in Refs. [31, 30, 34] therefore will not be discussed in detail in this article.

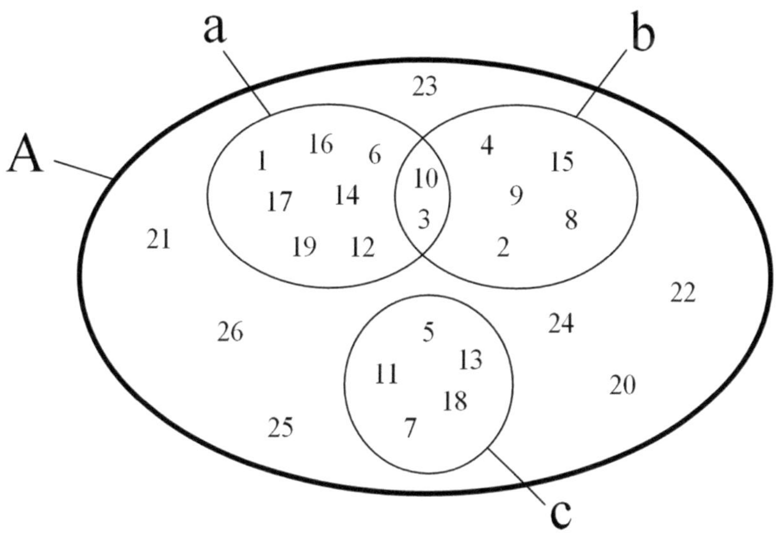

Figure 2. Social network relationship diagram.

GADM operates in a way that an influence is diffused to any social nodes given the existence of a physical link between the source node and the recipient node. Any influence diffused by GADM is considered successful if the influence propagated and acknowledged by the recipient social node. A number of enhancements will be carried out on GADM. These enhanced algorithms are trust-enhanced genetic algorithm diffusion model (T-GADM) that includes trust values calculated from the uncovering of trusted social node process into the influential diffusion and calculation process. In addition, domain values are included into the enhanced T-GADM resulting into the domain specified trust-enhanced genetic algorithm diffusion model (DST-GADM). On top of the diffusion of influence from trusted social nodes, DST-

GADM brings influence diffusion to a whole new level, where these influences will be diffused to target at recipient social nodes that shares the similar interest (or domains) with the source social node. The results generated by these algorithms are presented as probability values with a minimum value of 0 and a maximum value of 1, with an accuracy of 3 decimal points. Details of the algorithm design are discussed in Section4.

4. Algorithm design, development and implementation

This section discusses the design, development and implementation of the algorithms in this research. There are two algorithms to be discussed: trust-enabled generic algorithm diffusion model (T-GADM) and domain specified trust-enabled generic algorithm diffusion model (DST-GADM). These algorithms will be discussed in their respective subsections. It is also acknowledged that the operation of T-GADM and DST-GADM also rely on two additional sub-modules namely the enhanced text analysis (E-TA) with the presence of Trusted Social Node algorithm (TSN) and Virtual Social Node algorithm (VSN). These algorithms had been published in Refs. [30, 31, 34] therefore will not be discussed in this article.

4.1. Trust-enhanced Generic Algorithm Diffusion Model

Trust-enhanced Generic Algorithm Diffusion Model (T-GADM) is the enhanced algorithm version from generic algorithm diffusion model (GADM) where the source social node's trust value is taken into consideration when calculating the recipient social node's influence acceptance. The likelihood of a social node accepting an influence given the trusted source node is calculated by the application of certainty factor that measures the belief or disbelief conditional probabilities $\Pr(A_i|T)$ as illustrated in Eq. (2).

$$\Pr(A_i|T) = \frac{\Pr(T|C_i)\Pr(A)}{\Pr(T|C_i)\Pr(A) + \Pr(T|\neg C_i)\Pr(\neg A)} \tag{2}$$

Where:

- $\Pr(A_i|T)$: Chance of having an influence accepted by the recipient (A_i) given a trusted source (T). This is what the algorithm wants to calculate.
- $\Pr(T|C_i)$: Chance of having a trusted social node (T) given that it shows significant interactive consistency.
- $\Pr(A)$: Chance of having a recipient node to accept an influence.
- $\Pr(\neg A)$: Chance of having a recipient node to ***not*** accept an influence.
- $\Pr(T|\neg C_i)$: Chance of having a trusted social node (T) given that does not show significant interactive consistency.

The results generated from Eq. (3) are then used to evaluate the certainty factor that the influence has been successfully ingested. This is achieved by applying Eq. (3) as measure-of-belief and Eq. (4) for measure-of-disbelief, then finally calculating the certainty values by applying Eq. (5).

$$\mathrm{MB}(H_{accept}|E_{trust}) = \frac{\max[\Pr(A|T), \Pr(\alpha)] - \Pr(\alpha)}{1 - \Pr(\alpha)} \tag{3}$$

$$\mathrm{MD}(H_{accept}|E_{trust}) = \frac{\min[\Pr(A|T), \Pr(\alpha)] - \Pr(\alpha)}{1 - \Pr(\alpha)} \tag{4}$$

$$\mathrm{CF} = \frac{\mathrm{MB}(H_{accept}|E_{trust}) - \mathrm{MD}(H_{accept}|E_{trust})}{1 - \min[\mathrm{MB}(H_{accept}|E_{trust}), \mathrm{MD}(H_{accept}|E_{trust})]} \tag{5}$$

Eqs. (4)–(6) calculate the following parameters:

- PrAT: The probability of acceptance given the trust variance of a source node.
- MB_HaEt: The strength (measure) of belief the node will accept the influence.
- MD_HaEt: The strength (measure) of disbelief the node will accept the influence.
- cf: Certainty factor grouping of the current evaluating node.
- success: Describes the successfulness of the node being influenced. This criterion only applies if the threshold value is set prior to the evaluation. There is no specification on what the threshold value should be used. The threshold value is chosen based on the assessor's preferred influential range.

The following pseudocode illustrates the implementation of the T-GADM influential diffusion algorithm.

```
START
//Eqn ver 1 w/trust (Baysean Prop)
FUCNTION probability_v1(St,Ra)
Set PrAT = ((Ra * St) + St)/2;
return round(PrAT, 4);
END FUNCTION
//Eqn ver 2 w/trust (Enhanced Baysean)
FUNCTION probability_v2(St,Ra)
Set notRa = 1 - Ra;
Set notSt = 1 - St;
Set PrAT = ((Ra * St)/((Ra * St) + (notRa * notSt))) *
(1 - 0.13);
return round(PrAT, 4);
END FUNCTION
FUNCTION belief(const,PrAT,St,Ra)
Set MB_HaEt = ((max(PrAT,constant)) - constant)/(1 - constant);
return round(MB_HaEt, 4);
END FUNCTION
FUNCTION disbelief(const,PrAT,St,Ra)
Set MD_HaEt = ((min(PrAT, constant)) - constant)/(0 - constant);
return round(MD_HaEt, 4);
```

```
END FUNCTION
FUNCTION cf(MB_HaEt,MD_HaEt){
Set cf = (MB_HaEt - MD_HaEt)/(1 - (min(MB_HaEt, MD_HaEt)));
return round(cf, 4);
END FUNCTION
//Check Threshold
FUNCTION checkThresh(value,threshold){
IF input >= threshold
return 'accepted';
ELSE
return 'rejected';
END IF
END FUNCTION
END
```

4.2. Domain specified trust-enhanced generic algorithm diffusion model

This research also investigates the application of domain-related trusted social nodes in order to examine whether this will further increase the rate of successfully influenced social nodes on a social network platform. Domain in this research represents the interest groups a social node involves or participates in. Domain specified analysis is an extended module from the T-GADM. In the domain specified trust influence diffusion algorithm, an additional step that uncovers domains of each social node from the dataset is needed. All the domain relationship links harvested are illustrated as a conceptual diagram in **Figure 3**.

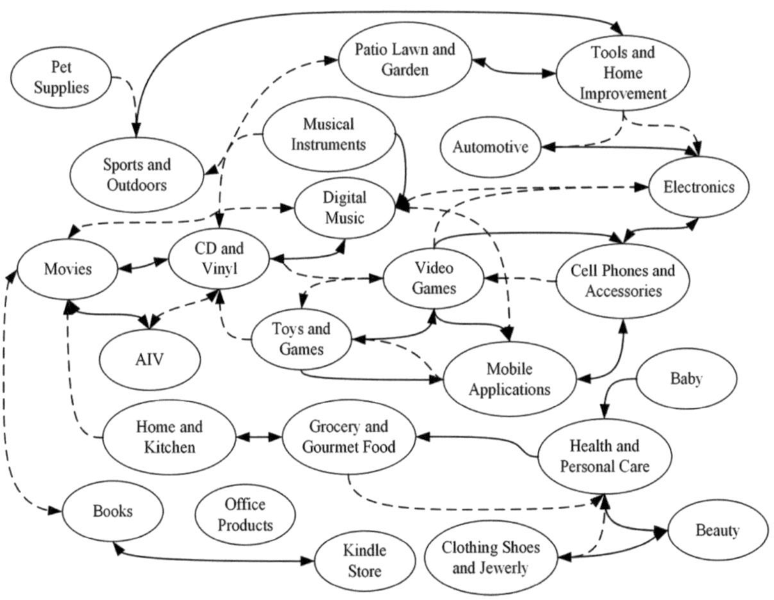

Figure 3. Harvested domains and domain links for domain specified trust influential maximization conceptual diagram.

http://dx.doi.org/10.5772/67021

The relationship between two domains is calculated by applying the concept mapping [35, 36] and weighing technique [37] where domain relationships are classified into three tiers:

- **Domain major** (*node*)—Is a form of specification or excellency to which a variable formally commits or inherits. Any domain can be a domain major, but only one domain can be the domain major at any given time.
- **Level 2 domain** (*solid line*)—Consist of entities that are directly correlate to the domain major (part of, extension of, subset) but do not serve as a domain major at point of analysis.
- **Domain Minor** (*dashed line*)—Consist of entities that are mostly not directly correlate to the domain major nor the second-order domain, but domain may consist of certain entities that portray traits and characteristics that relate to the domain major.

Each harvested domain, domain relationship links and domain relationship weights are then indexed using Domain ID (Domain Identity represented by a value) (as seen in **Table 2**).

Domain major		Level 2 domain		Domain minor	
ID	Weight	ID	Weight	ID	Weight
[01]	1.0	[16]	0.7821	[06]	0.3237
[02]	1.0	[10]	0.6762	–	
[03]	1.0	–		[12]	0.2997
[04]	1.0	[08]	0.8967	[12]	0.5521
[05]	1.0	[14]	0.6887	[16]	0.2194
[06]	1.0	[09]	0.4571	[01]	0.2857
		[16]	0.3321	[24]	0.1756
[07]	1.0	[10]	0.3123	[24]	0.2752
		[15]	0.5231		
[08]	1.0	[04]	0.6774	[12]	0.5882
[09]	1.0	[06]	0.7987	[15]	0.1725
				[10]	0.2141
				[16]	0.2365
[10]	1.0	[02]	0.2379	[09]	0.1423
		[07]	0.2656		
[11]	1.0	[13]	0.4597	[12]	0.2178
[12]	1.0	[11]	0.2287	–	
		[04]	0.3212		
		[08]	0.3101		
[13]	1.0	[11]	0.3427	[16]	0.1563
[14]	1.0	[05]	0.5638	–	

Domain major		Level 2 domain		Domain minor	
ID	Weight	ID	Weight	ID	Weight
[15]	1.0	[07]	0.8469	[09]	0.2112
				[23]	0.1211
[16]	1.0	[01]	0.5485	[09]	0.1653
		[06]	0.2324	[05]	0.1536
[17]	1.0	[09]	0.4439	[06]	0.2846
[18]	1.0	–		–	
[19]	1.0	[22]	0.4575	[21]	0.2133
[20]	1.0	–		[19]	0.1556
[21]	1.0	[22]	0.3354	[19]	0.1757
[22]	1.0	[19]	0.4121	[10]	0. 2675
				[02]	0.1294
[23]	1.0	[24]	0.3216	[06]	0.1128
		[15]	0.2144		
[24]	1.0	[15]	0.4174	[23]	0.1127
		[07]	0.2152	[10]	0.1216

Table 2. Weighted domain specified referent table.

Domain specified trust influence uses Eq. (6) for social influential acceptance-related calculations.

$$\mathrm{DwPr}(\mathrm{A}_i|\mathrm{T}) = \frac{[\Pr(\mathrm{A}_i|\mathrm{T}) + \Pr(\mathrm{A}_i|\mathrm{T})(Dmjr + \sum\cap L2 + \sum\cap Dmnr)]}{1 + \Pr(\mathrm{A}_i|\mathrm{T})(Dmjr + \sum\cap L2 + \sum\cap Dmnr)} \tag{6}$$

Where

- $\mathrm{DwPr}(\mathrm{A_i}|\mathrm{T})$: Chance of having an influence accepted by the recipient (A_i) given a trusted source (T) with the presence of certain domain entities (Dw).
- $\Pr(\mathrm{A_i}|\mathrm{T})$: Chance of having an influence accepted by the recipient ($\mathrm{A_i}$) given a trusted source (T). This is what the algorithm previously calculated.
- Dmjr: Represents the weight inherited by the domain major. In this research, since the domain major represents absolute identical relationship to the domain inherited by the node in analysis, therefore the concept weight between the node in analysis and domain major is 1.0.
- $\sum\bigcap L2$: Represents the summation of all weights of intersected level 2 domains with the domain inherited by the node in analysis.

- $\sum\bigcap$ *Dmnr*: Represents the summation of all weights of intersected domain minors with the domain inherited by the node in analysis.

The following pseudocode illustrates the implementation of the DST-GADM influential diffusion algorithm

```
START
Import domains as domainsCache
//Eqn ver 3 w/trust and domain (Enhanced Baysean)
FUNCTION probability_v3(St,Ra,links,levels)
Set mjr = 0;
Set l2 = 0;
Set mnr = 0;
//Explode node links
Set links = explode('|', links);
Set major = links.getLastElement();
//Find associative domains
FOREACH domainsCache as key and payload
IF payload.get['major'] == major
Set use = domainsCache.get[key];
END IF
END FOREACH
//Prep traverse levels
Set traverseArrays = [];
IF levels == 1
Set mjr = (float) mjr(use,links);
ELSE IF levels == 2
Set mjr = (float) mjr(use,links);
Set l2 = (float) level2(use,links);
ELSE IF levels == 3
Set mjr = (float) mjr(use,links);
Set l2 = (float) level2(use,links);
Set mnr = (float) mnr(use,links);
END IF
Set notRa = 1 - Ra;
Set notSt = 1 - St;
Set prob = ((Ra * St)/((Ra * St) + (notRa * notSt))) *
(1 - 0.13);
Set PrAT = (prob + (prob * mjr) + (prob * l2) + (prob * mnr))/
(1 + (prob * mjr) + (prob * l2) + (prob * mnr));
return round(PrAT, 4);
END FUNCTION
//Calculate domain weightages (returns calculated values)
```

```
FUNCTION mjr(use,links)
IF links.getLastElemet() == use.get['major'])
Set payloads = use.get['payload'];
return payloads['majorWeight'];
ELSE
return 0;
END IF
END FUNCTION
FUNCTION level2(use,links)
Set payloads = use.get['payload'];
Set payloads = payloads.get['level2'];
Set cumulativeWeight = 0;
FOREACH links as link
FOREACH payloads as payload
IF payload.get['domainID'] == link
Set cumulativeWeight += payload.get['weight'];
END IF
END FOREACH
END FOREACH
return cumulativeWeight;
END FUNCTION
FUNCTION mnr(use,links)
Set payloads = use.get['payload'];
Set payloads = payloads.get['minor'];
Set cumulativeWeight = 0;
FOREACH links as link
FOREACH payloads as payload
IF payload.get['domainID'] == link
Set cumulativeWeight += payload.get['weight'];
END IF
END FOREACH
END FOREACH
return cumulativeWeight;
END FUNCTION
```

4.3. Acceptance threshold

Threshold value represents the level of certainty both the source node and the recipient node must adhere to. By increasing the threshold value means increasing the quality of influencing messages and the level of trust propagated from the source social node, hence it potentially reducing the number of successfully influenced social nodes. Since there is no common specification on what threshold value should be used and the values often depend on the researcher's preference, threshold value used in this research is set to neutral or zero (0).

5. Results and discussion

In this article, results generated from the proposed genetic algorithm diffusion model (GADM), enhanced genetic algorithm diffusion model (T-GADM) and domain specified trust-enhanced genetic algorithm diffusion model (DST-GADM) will be compared and discussed respectively. **Figure 4** shows the difference between results generated from the base algorithm and the trust-enhanced algorithm on the effects of the rates of successfully influenced social nodes within the simulated social networking environment, whereas **Figure 5** illustrates the successful influence acceptance rates with threshold value set to default (0).

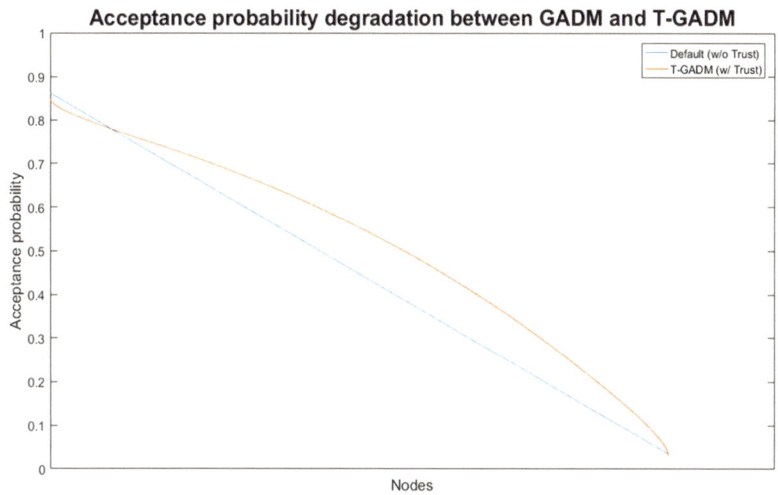

Figure 4. Acceptance probability for GADM vs. T-GADM.

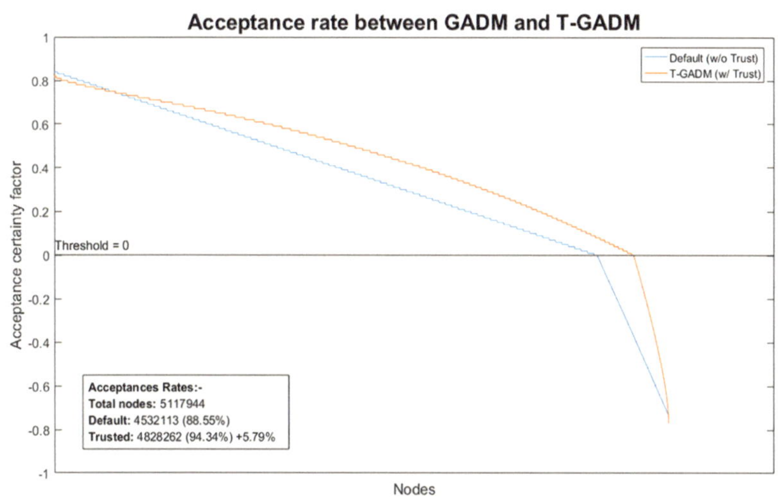

Figure 5. Acceptance statistics for GADM vs. T-GADM.

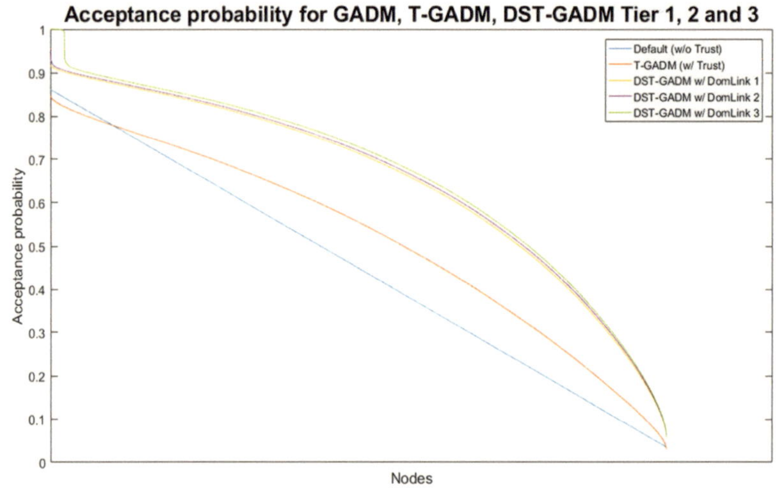

Figure 6. Acceptance probability for GADM vs. T-GADM vs. DST-GADM Tier 1, 2 and 3.

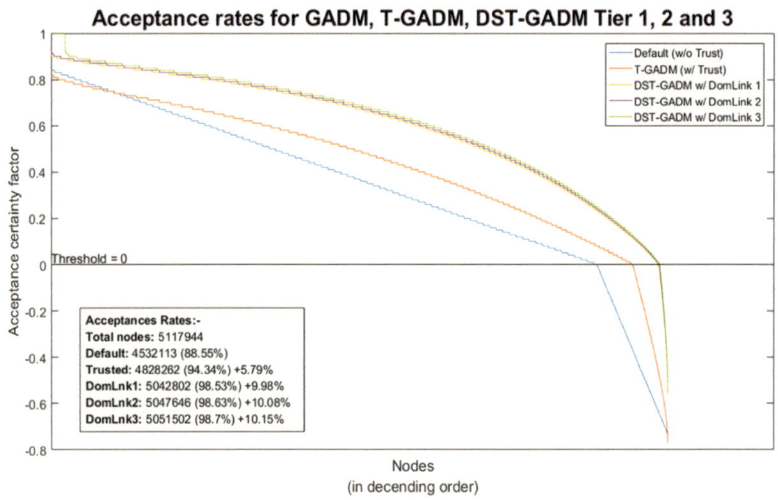

Figure 7. Acceptance rates for GADM vs. T-GADM vs. DST-GADM Tier 1, 2 and 3.

All percentages presented in this section are calculated by averaging the differences on the rate of successfully influenced social nodes between two or more algorithms where the GADM algorithm will serve as the benchmark. The analysis showed that by comparing results generated between GADM (base algorithm without trusted social node) and T-GADM (enhanced algorithm with trusted social node), the T-GADM algorithm yields 5.79% increment on the rate of successfully influenced social nodes compared to GADM. Such increment on the rate of successfully influenced social nodes is because social nodes that are trustworthy have higher tendency of being accepted by other social nodes; therefore, influence spread by these trustworthy social nodes may strongly be accepted. Furthering the analysis, results generated show that the

DST-GADM (domain specified trust influence) yields a further 4% improvement on the rate of successfully influenced social nodes when it is compared to T-GADM (enhanced algorithm with trusted social node) and about 10% improvement on the rate of successfully influenced social nodes when it is compared to GADM (base algorithm without trusted social node). Such improvement is expected since it is said that trusted social nodes that share the similar interest would be better at influencing social nodes within the interest group. Analysis results are illustrated in **Figures 6** and **7**. Both results also concluded the hypothesis presented in this article where it is said that social trust plays an important role in influential propagation, and it is able to increase the rate of success in influencing other social nodes in a social network.

6. Conclusion

The outcome of this research has shown considerable increments in the rate of successfully influenced social nodes between 5.58% and 5.89% with the presence of social trust within social nodes. The result has also shown that the rate of successfully influenced social nodes can be further improved with the introduction of domain specified trust with an additional increment between 0.02 and 4.31%. The results also suggest that the rate of successfully influenced social nodes may vary when different levels of domain relationship links are introduced such as the presence of domain majors, level 2 domains and domain minors, although it is also seen that some of social nodes may not be affected by the additional levels of domain relationship links. It is also found that some social nodes' acceptance probability dropped while comparing between the base algorithm and the trust enabled algorithm. This outcome is aligned with our initial expectation because the drop in certain social nodes' acceptance probability can be caused by source nodes with lower trust values. On the whole, the dataset used in this research had an average increment value of 9% on the rate of successfully influenced social nodes with the application of trusted social node and domain-specified trust, including domains from all three tiers of domain relationship links classified for this research. Although the incremental percentages is insignificant, but consider the size of the dataset is large and the characteristics of different dataset used in the research may influence the performance, the marginal improvement found needs to be taken into consideration in this context. Finally, research also foresees two possible future researches that can be applied to further enhance the social nodes influence strength and the acceptance results obtained from this research. These applications include distance weighted trust and trust value down the lane.

Author details

Yap Hock Yeow and Lim Tong-Ming*

*Address all correspondence to: tongmingl@sunway.edu.my

Faculty of Science and Technology, Sunway University, Petaling Jaya, Malaysia

References

[1] I. T. Union, "Internet Users (Per 100 People) 1981–2014," The World Bank, December 2014. [Online]. Available: http://data.worldbank.org/indicator/IT.NET.USER.P2. [Accessed 2 July 2015].

[2] A. Gesenhues, "Survey: 90% Of Customers Say Buying Decisions Are Influenced By Online Reviews," Marketing Land, United States, 2013.

[3] H. Paquette, "Social Media as a Marketing Tool: A Literature Review," University of Rhode Island, United States, 2013.

[4] K. Quesenberry, "Social Media Is Too Important to Be Left to the Marketing Department," Harvard Business Publishing, United States, 2016.

[5] M. Ewing, "71% More Likely to Purchase Based on Social Media Referrals," HubSpot, United States, 2011.

[6] A. Josang, R. Ismail and C. Byod, "A Survey of Trust and Reputation Systems for Online Service Provision," in Decision Support Systems, Amsterdam, 2007.

[7] J. Caverlee, L. Liu and S. Webb, "The SocialTrust framework for trusted social information management: Architecture and algorithms," Journal of Information Science, vol. 180, no. 1, pp. 95–112, 2010.

[8] E. Hargittai, L. Fullerton, E. Menchen-Trevino and K. Thomas, "Trust online: young adults' evaluation of web content," International Journal of Communication, vol. 4, no. 1, pp. 468–494, 2010.

[9] P. Resnick and R. Zeckhauser, "Trust among strangers in internet transactions: empirical analysis of ebay's reputation system," Advances in Applied Microeconomics, vol. 11, no. 2, pp. 127–157, 2002.

[10] S. Hendrickson, "Case Study: How Content Diffuses Through Different Social Networks," Social Media Today, United States, 2013.

[11] H. Leonard, "The Fascinating Spread of Content Through Social Networks," Business Insider, United Kingdom, 2013.

[12] J. Tierney, "Social Media Helps Police, Cities Spread Information," Daily Herald, Utah, 2013.

[13] B. Marcus, F. Machilek and A. Schutz, "Personality in cyberspace: personal Web sites as media for personality expressions and impressions," Journal of Personality and Social Psychology, vol. 90, no. 6, pp. 1014–1031, 2006.

[14] A. Renninger and W. Shumar, Building Virtual Communities: Learning and Change in Cyberspace, United Kingdom: Cambridge University Press, 2002.

[15] R. Morgan and S. Hunt, "The commitment-trust theory of relationship marketing," Journal of Marketing, vol. 58, no. 1, pp. 20–38, 1994.

[16] D. Gefen, E. Karahanna and D. Straub, "Trust and TAM in online shopping: an integrated model," MIS Quarterly, vol. 27, no. 1, pp. 51–90, 2003.

[17] E. Yildirim, "The effects of user comments on e-trust: an application on consumer electronics," Journal of Economics, Business and Management, vol. 1, no. 4, pp. 360–364, 2013.

[18] J. Weiseberg, D. Te'eni and L. Arman, "Past purchase and intention to purchase in e-commerce: the mediation of social presence and trust," Internet Research, vol. 21, no. 1, pp. 82–96, 2011.

[19] M. Gustavsson and A.-M. Johansson, "Consumer Trust in E-commerce," in Kristianstad University, Sweden, 2006.

[20] D. Gambetta, "Can We Trust Trust?," in Basil Blackwell, Oxford, 1988.

[21] R. Falcone and C. Castelfranchi, "Social Trust: A Cognitive Approach," in Kluwer, Netherlands, 2001.

[22] H. McKnight, "What trust means in e-commerce customer relationships: an interdisciplinary conceptual typology," International Journal of Electronic Commerce, United States, 2002.

[23] J. McAuley, P. Rahul and J. Leskovec, "Inferring networks of substitutable and complementary products," in SIGKDD, Sydney, 2015.

[24] J. McAuley, C. Targett, Q. Shi and A. v. d. Hengel, "Image-based recommendations on styles and substitutes," in SIGIR Santiago - Chile, Santiago, 2015.

[25] M. Richardson, R. Agrawal and P. Domingos, "Trust management for the semantic web," in International Semantic Web Conference, Florida, 2003.

[26] M. Q. Hu and B. Liu, "Mining and summarizing customer reviews," in ACM International Conference on Knowledge Discovery and Data Mining, New York, 2004.

[27] S.-M. Kim and E. Hovy, "Determining the sentiment of opinions," in International Conference on Computational Linguistics, Stroudsburg, 2004.

[28] P. Bo and L. Lee, "Seeing stars: Exploiting class relationships for sentiment categorization with respect to rating scales," in Annual Meeting on Association for Computational Linguistics, Stroudsburg, 2005.

[29] T. Wilson and J. Wiebe, "Recognizing strong and weak opinion," Computational Intelligence, vol. 22, no. 2, pp. 73–99, 2006.

[30] Y. Hock-Yeow and L. Tong-Ming, "An evaluation and enhancement of the sentiment oriented opinion mining technique using opinion scoring," in International Conference on Innovation and Sustainability 2015, Chiang Mai, 2015.

[31] Y. Hock-Yeow and L. Tong-Ming, "An analysis of opinion variation of social text in the trusted social node identification," in American Scientific Publishers Advance Science Letters, Sabah, Malaysia, 2016.

[32] D. Kempe, J. Kleinberg and E. Tardos, "influential nodes in a diffusion model for social networks," in Proceedings of the 32nd International conference on Automata, Languages and Programming, Berlin, 2005.

[33] D. Kempe, J. Kleinberg and E. Tardos, "Maximizing the spread of influence through a social network," in Proceedings of the ninth ACM SIGKDD international conference on Knowledge discovery and data mining, New York, 2003.

[34] Y. Hock-Yeow and L. Tong-Ming, "Trusted Social Node: Evaluating the Effect of Trust and Trust Variance to Maximize Social Influence in a Multilevel Social Node Influential Diffusion Model," in Springer Lecture Notes in Computer Science, Beijing, 2016.

[35] J. Novak, "The Theory Underlying Concept Maps and How to Construct and Use Them," Institute for Human and Machine Cognition, United States, 2006.

[36] J. Novak, "Learning, creating, and using knowledge: concept maps as facilitative tools in schools and corporations," Journal of e-Learning and Knowledge Society, vol. 6, no. 3, pp. 21–30, 2010.

[37] C. Lin and R. Nayak, "A case study of failure mode analysis with text mining methods," in 2nd International Workshop on Integrating Artificial Intelligence and Data Mining, Australia, 2007.

Chapter 3

A Distributed Computing Architecture for the Large-Scale Integration of Renewable Energy and Distributed Resources in Smart Grids

Ignacio Aravena, Anthony Papavasiliou and
Alex Papalexopoulos

Additional information is available at the end of the chapter

http://dx.doi.org/10.5772/67791

Abstract

We present a distributed computing architecture for smart grid management, composed of two applications at two different levels of the grid. At the high voltage level, we optimize operations using a stochastic unit commitment (SUC) model with hybrid time resolution. The SUC problem is solved with an asynchronous distributed subgradient method, for which we propose stepsize scaling and fast initialization techniques. The asynchronous algorithm is implemented in a high-performance computing cluster and benchmarked against a deterministic unit commitment model with exogenous reserve targets in an industrial scale test case of the Central Western European system (679 buses, 1037 lines, and 656 generators). At the distribution network level, we manage demand response from small clients through distributed stochastic control, which enables harnessing residential demand response while respecting the desire of consumers for control, privacy, and simplicity. The distributed stochastic control scheme is successfully tested on a test case with 10,000 controllable devices. Both applications demonstrate the potential for efficiently managing flexible resources in smart grids and for systematically coping with the uncertainty and variability introduced by renewable energy.

Keywords: smart grids, stochastic programming, asynchronous distributed algorithm, stochastic control, demand response

1. Introduction

The progressive integration of renewable energy resources, demand response, energy storage, electric vehicles, and other distributed resources in electric power grids that has been taking place worldwide in recent years is transforming power systems and resulting in numerous operational challenges, including uncertainty of supply availability, distributed storage management, real-time coordination of distributed energy resources, and changing directions of flow in distribution networks. These challenges demand a shift of the traditional centralized power system operations paradigm toward the smart grid paradigm [1], where distributed computing and control stand out as a promising technology with the potential of achieving operations with optimal performance.

The academic literature includes various applications of distributed computing in power system operations, including long- and mid-term planning, short-term scheduling, state estimation and monitoring, real-time control, and simulation [2–5]. Early studies pointed out several challenges related to communications and the heterogeneous characteristics of distributed computing systems, which needed to be addressed first in order to implement distributed computing applications. Nowadays, standard communication protocols are a mature technology and most current distributed computing resources can perform a broad range of operations. Such advances in distributed computing technology have paved the way for developing and implementing scalable distributed algorithms for power systems.

The prevailing industry view, as we move forward into the future smart grid, is that it will entail: (i) broadcasting of dynamic prices or other information and (ii) telemetry backhaul to market participants. In the proposed model, distributed energy resource aggregators are often regarded as transaction brokers between end customers and various upstream market participants. The "failure-free market" design for a pure market-driven solution under this paradigm has been elusive, despite decades of research and development. In this chapter, we analyze the deployment of distributed computing as an enabling tool for managing the short-term operations of smart grids in two levels:

- At the level of the high-voltage grid, we centrally optimize operations using a stochastic unit commitment (SUC) model, which endogenously allocates reserve capacity by explicitly modeling uncertainty. Specifically, we present an asynchronous distributed algorithm for solving SUC, which extends the asynchronous algorithm proposed in Ref. [6] in three aspects: (i) we propose a hybrid approach for modeling quarterly dispatch decisions alongside hourly commitment decisions; (ii) we introduce a stepsize scaling on the iterative method to diminish the error due to asynchronous execution; and (iii) we propose two methods for a faster initialization of the algorithm. The asynchronous algorithm is implemented in a high-performance computing (HPC) cluster and benchmarked against a deterministic unit commitment model with exogenous reserve targets (DUCR). We find that distributed computing allows solving SUC within the same time frame required for solving DUCR.

- At the level of the distribution grid, we rely on stochastic distributed control to manage consumer devices using the ColorPower architecture [7–9], which enables harnessing flexible residential demand response while respecting the desire of consumers for control, privacy, and simplicity. The ColorPower control approach is inspired by the very automatic cooperative protocols that govern Internet communications. These protocols represent a distributed and federated control paradigm, in which information and decision-making authority remain local, yet global system stability is ensured.

http://dx.doi.org/10.5772/67791

Centralized clearing at the high-voltage grid level and distributed clearing at the distribution grid level can be integrated in a cooptimization framework, as recently proposed by Caramanis et al. [10]. These two applications of distributed computing in power system operations demonstrate the potential to fully harness the flexibility of the grid and smoothly integrate large shares of renewable and other distributed energy resources in power systems without deteriorating the quality of service delivered to consumers.

The rest of the chapter is organized as follows: Section 2 introduces the deterministic and stochastic unit commitment problems. Section 3 proposes an asynchronous algorithm for solving SUC and presents numerical experiments on a network of realistic scale. Section 4 presents the ColorPower architecture for managing demand response in the distribution grid and demonstrates its capability through a numerical experiment. Finally, Section 5 concludes the chapter.

2. High-voltage power grid optimization models

2.1. Overview

Operations of the high-voltage power grid are typically scheduled in two stages: (i) day-ahead scheduling, where operations are planned based on forecast conditions for the system and the on/off status of slow generators is fixed and (ii) real-time scheduling, where system operators balance the system for the actual conditions using the available flexibility in the system. Models for short-term scheduling are solved on a daily basis, and they occupy a central role in clearing power markets and operating power systems.

Until recently, power system operators have relied on deterministic short-term scheduling models with reserve margins to secure the system against load forecast errors and outages [11–14]. The integration of renewable energy sources has placed these practices under question because they ignore the inherent uncertainty of renewable energy supply, thereby motivating system operators and researchers to look for systematic methods to address uncertainty in real-time operations. A consistent methodology for mitigating the impacts of renewable energy uncertainty—and operational uncertainty in general—is stochastic programming. Stochastic models for short-term scheduling (i.e., SUC models) were originally considered in the seminal work of Takriti et al. [15] and Carpentier et al. [16], as an approach for mitigating demand uncertainty and generator outages. Subsequently, numerous variants of the SUC model have been proposed, which differ on the number of stages, the source of uncertainty, the representation of uncertainty, and the solution methods that are used. See Ref. [17] and references therein for a recent survey.

In the present work, we use the deterministic and stochastic unit commitment models for day-ahead scheduling presented in Sections 3.1 and 3.2. The proposed models differ from previously proposed models in the literature in which they use hybrid time resolution: hourly commitment decisions (u, v, w and z) and 15-min dispatch decisions (p, r and f). This formulation allows modeling subhourly phenomena, which have been shown to be important for the operation of systems with significant levels of renewable energy integration [18].

2.2. Deterministic unit commitment with exogenous reserve targets

Using the notation provided in the beginning of the section, we model deterministic unit commitment with reserves (DUCR) as the minimization problem Eqs. (1)–(9).

$$\min_{p,r,u,v,f} \sum_{g \in G} \Big(\sum_{\tau \in T_{60}} (K_g u_{g,\tau} + S_g v_{g,\tau}) + \sum_{t \in T_{15}} C_g(p_{g,t}) \Big) \quad (1)$$

$$\text{s.t.} \sum_{g \in G(n)} p_{g,t} + \sum_{l \in L(\cdot,n)} f_{l,t} + \overline{\xi}_{n,t} \geq D_{n,t} + \sum_{l \in L(n,\cdot)} f_{l,t} \;\; \forall n \in N, t \in T_{15} \quad (2)$$

$$\sum_{g \in G(a)} r^2_{g,t} \geq \mathcal{R}^2_a, \;\; \sum_{g \in G(N(a))} (r^2_{g,t} + r^3_{g,t}) \geq \mathcal{R}^2_a + \mathcal{R}^3_a \;\; \forall a \in A, t \in T_{15} \quad (3)$$

$$f_{l,t} = B_l \Big(\theta_{n(l),t} - \theta_{m(l),t} \Big), \; -F^-_l \leq f_{l,t} \leq F^+_l \;\; \forall l \in L, t \in T_{15} \quad (4)$$

$$P^-_g u_{g,\tau(t)} \leq p_{g,t}, \; p_{g,t} + r^2_{g,t} + r^3_{g,t} \leq P^+_g u_{g,\tau(t)} \;\; \forall g \in G_{SLOW}, t \in T_{15} \quad (5)$$

$$P^-_g u_{g,\tau(t)} \leq p_{g,t}, \; p_{g,t} + r^2_{g,t} \leq P^+_g u_{g,\tau(t)}, \; p_{g,t} + r^2_{g,t} + r^3_{g,t} \leq P^+_g \;\; \forall g \in G \backslash G_{SLOW}, t \in T_{15} \quad (6)$$

$$-TL_g + (TL_g - R^-_g)\, u_{g,\tau(t)} \leq p_{g,t} - p_{g,t-1} \;\; \forall g \in G, t \in T_{15} \quad (7)$$

$$\begin{aligned} p_{g,t} + \frac{15}{\Delta T_2} r^2_{g,t} - p_{g,t-1} &\leq TL_g - (TL_g - R^+_g)\, u_{g,\tau(t-1)}, \\ p_{g,t} + \frac{15}{\Delta T_3} (r^2_{g,t} + r^3_{g,t}) - p_{g,t-1} &\leq TL_g - (TL_g - R^+_g)\, u_{g,\tau(t-1)} \;\; \forall g \in G, t \in T_{15} \end{aligned} \quad (8)$$

$$u_{g,\tau} \in \{0,1\}, v_{g,\tau} \in \{0,1\} \;\; \forall g \in G, \tau \in T_{60} \quad (9)$$

The objective function Eq. (1) corresponds to the total operating cost, composed by the no-load cost, the startup cost, and the production cost. Constraints Eq. (2) enforce nodal power balance, while allowing for production shedding. Demand shedding can be included in the present formulation as having a very expensive generator connected to each bus. Eq. (3) enforces the reserve margins on each area of the system, allowing for reserve cascading (secondary reserve capacity can be used to provide tertiary reserve). Eq. (4) models DC power flow constraints in terms of bus angles and thermal limits of transmission lines.

The feasible production set of thermal generators is described by Eqs. (5)–(9). Production and reserve provision limits are expressed as Eq. (5) for slow generators, that can provide reserves only when they are online, and as Eq. (6) for the remaining set of generators, which can provide secondary reserves when they are online and tertiary reserves both when they are online and offline. Ramp rate constraints Eqs. (7)–(8) are based on the formulation provided by Frangioni et al. [19]. Ramp-up rate constraints Eq. (8) enforce, in addition to the ramp-up rate limit on production, that there is enough ramping capability between periods $t-1$ and t to ramp-up $r^2_{g,t}$ MW within ΔT_2 minutes (which can be used to provide secondary reserve), and to ramp-up $r^2_{g,t} + r^3_{g,t}$ MW within ΔT_3 minutes (which can be used to provide tertiary reserve). Constraints Eq. (9) enforce minimum up and down times, as proposed by Rajan and Takriti [20].

Boundary conditions of the problem are modeled by allowing the time indices to cycle within the horizon, in other words, for any commitment variable $x_{\cdot,\tau}$ with $\tau < 1$, we define $x_{\cdot,\tau} := x_{\cdot,((\tau-1) \bmod |T_{60}|+1)}$. Similarly, for any dispatch variable $x_{\cdot,t}$ with $t < 1$ or $t > |T_{15}|$, we define $x_{\cdot,t} := x_{\cdot,((t-1) \bmod |T_{15}|+1)}$. In this fashion, we model initial conditions ($\tau < 1$, $t < 1$) and restrain end effects of the model ($\tau = |T_{60}|$, $t = |T_{15}|$), simultaneously. In practical cases, initial conditions are given by the current operating conditions and end effects are dealt with by using an extended look-ahead horizon.

2.3. Two-stage stochastic unit commitment and scenario decomposition

Following Papavasiliou et al. [21], we formulate SUC as the two-stage stochastic program of Eqs. (10)–(17).

$$\min_{\substack{p,u,v,f\\ w,z}} \sum_{s\in S}\pi_s \sum_{g\in G}\Big(\sum_{\tau\in T_{60}}(K_g u_{g,s,\tau} + S_g v_{g,s,\tau}) + \sum_{t\in T_{15}} C_g(p_{g,s,t})\Big) \tag{10}$$

$$\text{s.t.} \sum_{g\in G(n)} p_{g,s,t} + \sum_{l\in L(\cdot,n)} f_{l,s,t} + \xi_{n,s,t} \geq D_{n,t} + \sum_{l\in L(n,\cdot)} f_{l,s,t} \;\; \forall n\in N,\; s\in S, t\in T_{15} \tag{11}$$

$$f_{l,s,t} = B_l\left(\theta_{n(l),s,t} - \theta_{m(l),s,t}\right),\; -F_l^- \leq f_{l,s,t} \leq F_l^+ \;\; \forall l\in L, s\in S, t\in T_{15} \tag{12}$$

$$P_g^- u_{g,s,\tau(t)} \leq p_{g,s,t} \leq P_g^+ u_{g,s,\tau(t)} \;\; \forall g\in G,\; s\in S, t\in T_{15} \tag{13}$$

$$\begin{aligned} &-TL_g + (TL_g - R_g^-)\, u_{g,\tau(t)} \leq p_{g,s,t} - p_{g,s,t-1} \leq \\ &TL_g - (TL_g - R_g^+)\, u_{g,\tau(t-1)} \;\; \forall g\in G, s\in S, t\in T_{15} \end{aligned} \tag{14}$$

$$\begin{aligned} &v_{g,s,\tau} \geq u_{g,s,\tau} - u_{g,s,\tau}, \quad \sum_{\sigma=\tau-UT_g+1}^{\tau} v_{g,s,\sigma} \leq u_{g,s,\tau}, \quad \sum_{\sigma=\tau-DT_g+1}^{\tau} v_{g,s,\sigma} \leq 1 - u_{g,s,\tau-DT_g}, \\ &u_{g,s,\tau} \in \{0,1\},\; v_{g,s,\tau} \in \{0,1\} \;\; \forall g\in G,\; s\in S, \tau\in T_{60} \end{aligned} \tag{15}$$

$$\pi_s u_{g,s,\tau} = \pi_s w_{g,\tau} \rightarrow \mu_{g,s,\tau}, \pi_s v_{g,s,\tau} = \pi_s z_{g,\tau} \rightarrow \boldsymbol{\nu}_{g,s,\tau} \;\; \forall g\in G_{SLOW}, s\in S, \tau\in T_{60} \tag{16}$$

$$\begin{aligned} &z_{g,\tau} \geq w_{g,\tau} - w_{g,\tau}, \quad \sum_{\sigma=\tau-UT_g+1}^{\tau} z_{g,\sigma} \leq w_{g,\tau}, \quad \sum_{\sigma=\tau-DT_g+1}^{\tau} z_{g,\sigma} \leq 1 - w_{g,\tau-DT_g} \\ &w_{g,\tau} \in \{0,1\}, z_{g,\tau} \in \{0,1\} \;\; \forall g\in G, \tau\in T_{60} \end{aligned} \tag{17}$$

The objective function in Eq. (10) corresponds to the expected cost over the set of scenarios S, with associated probabilities π_s. Constraints in Eqs. (11)–(12) are analogous to Eqs. (2) and (4). No explicit reserve requirements are enforced in the stochastic unit commitment model, since reserves are endogenously determined by the explicit modeling of uncertainty. Consequently, generator constraints of the deterministic problem, Eqs. (5)–(10), become identical for all thermal generators and can be expressed as Eqs. (13)–(15). Nonanticipativity constraints Eq. (16) are formulated using state variables w and z for the commitment and startup decisions of slow thermal generators (first-stage decisions). We associate Lagrange multipliers μ and ν with nonanticipativity constraints. Constraints in Eq. (17) enforce minimum up and down times on unit commitment variables.

3. An asynchronous distributed algorithm for stochastic unit commitment

3.1. Scenario decomposition of the SUC problem

The SUC problem in Eqs. (10)–(17) grows linearly in size with the number of scenarios. Hence, SUC problems are in general of large scale, even for small system models. This motivated Takriti et al. [15] and Carpentier et al. [16] to rely on Lagrangian decomposition methods for solving the problem.

Recent SUC studies have focused on designing decomposition algorithms, capable of solving the problem in operationally acceptable time frames. Papavasiliou et al. [21] proposed a dual scenario decomposition scheme where the dual is solved using the subgradient method, and where the dual function is evaluated in parallel. Kim and Zavala [22] also used a dual scenario decomposition scheme, but solved the dual problem using a bundle method. Cheung et al. [23] present a parallel implementation of the progressive hedging algorithm of Rockafellar and Wets [24].

All previously mentioned parallel algorithms for SUC are synchronous algorithms, i.e., scenario subproblems are solved in parallel at each iteration of the decomposition method; however, it is necessary to solve all scenario subproblems before advancing to the next iteration. In cases where the solution times of subproblems differ significantly, synchronous algorithms lead to an under-utilization of the parallel computing infrastructure and a loss of parallel efficiency. We have found instances where the time required to evaluate subproblems for difficult scenarios is 75 times longer than the solution time for easy scenarios.

Aiming at overcoming the difficulties faced by synchronous algorithms, we propose an asynchronous distributed algorithm for solving SUC. The algorithm is based on the scenario decomposition scheme for SUC proposed in Ref. [21], where the authors relax the nonanticipativity constraints Eq. (16) and form the following Lagrangian dual problem

$$\max_{\mu, \nu} h_0(\boldsymbol{\mu}, \boldsymbol{\nu}) + \sum_{s \in S} h_s(\boldsymbol{\mu}_s, \boldsymbol{\nu}_s), \tag{18}$$

where $h_0(\boldsymbol{\mu}, \boldsymbol{\nu})$ and $h_s(\boldsymbol{\mu}_s, \boldsymbol{\nu}_s)$ are defined according to Eqs. (19) and (20), respectively. We use boldface to denote vectors and partial indexation of dual variables with respect to scenarios, so that $\boldsymbol{\mu}_s := [\mu_{g_1, s, 1} \cdots \mu_{g_{|G|}, s, 1}]^T$. The constraints within the infimum in Eq. (20) refer to constraints Eqs. (11)–(15) for scenario s (dropping the scenario indexation of variables).

$$h_0(\boldsymbol{\mu}, \boldsymbol{\nu}) := \inf_{w, z} \left\{ \sum_{g \in G_{SLOW}} \sum_{\tau \in T_{60}} \left(- \left(\sum_{s \in S} (\pi_s \boldsymbol{\mu}_{g, s, \tau}) \right) w_{g, \tau} - \left(\sum_{s \in S} (\pi_s \boldsymbol{\nu}_{g, s, \tau}) \right) z_{g, \tau} \right) \ : (17) \right\} \tag{19}$$

http://dx.doi.org/10.5772/67791

$$h_s(\boldsymbol{\mu}_s, \boldsymbol{\nu}_s) := \pi_s \inf_{p,u,v,f} \left\{ \begin{array}{c} \sum_{g \in G} \sum_{t \in T_{15}} C_g(p_{g,t}) + \sum_{g \in G \setminus G_{SLOW}} \sum_{\tau \in T_{60}} (K_g u_{g,\tau} + S_g v_{g,\tau}) + \\ \sum_{g \in G_{SLOW}} \sum_{\tau \in T_{60}} \left((K_g + \boldsymbol{\mu}_{g,s,\tau}) u_{g,\tau} + (S_g + \boldsymbol{\nu}_{g,s,\tau}) v_{g,\tau} \right) \ : (11s) - (15s) \end{array} \right\} \tag{20}$$

Both $h_0(\boldsymbol{\mu}, \boldsymbol{\nu})$ and $h_s(\boldsymbol{\mu}_s, \boldsymbol{\nu}_s)$ for all $s \in S$ are nondifferentiable convex functions. Evaluating $h_0(\boldsymbol{\mu}, \boldsymbol{\nu})$ amounts to solving a small integer programming problem, for the constraints of which we have a linear-size convex hull description [20]. Evaluating $h_s(\boldsymbol{\mu}_s, \boldsymbol{\nu}_s)$ amounts to solving a deterministic unit commitment (DUC) problem without reserve requirements, which is a mixed-integer linear program of potentially large scale for realistic system models. In practice, the run time for evaluating $h_s(\boldsymbol{\mu}_s, \boldsymbol{\nu}_s)$ for any s and any dual multipliers is at least two orders of magnitude greater than the run time for evaluating $h_0(\boldsymbol{\mu}, \boldsymbol{\nu})$.

The proposed distributed algorithm exploits the characteristics of $h_0(\boldsymbol{\mu}, \boldsymbol{\nu})$ and $h_s(\boldsymbol{\mu}_s, \boldsymbol{\nu}_s)$ in order to maximize Eq. (18) and compute lower bounds on the optimal SUC solution, while recovering feasible nonanticipative commitment schedules with associated expected costs (upper bounds to the optimal SUC solution). The dual maximization algorithm is inspired by the work of Nedić et al. on asynchronous incremental subgradient methods [25].

3.2. Dual maximization and primal recovery

For simplicity, assume that we have $1 + DP + PP$ available parallel processors which can all access a shared memory space. We allocate one processor to coordinate the parallel execution and manage the shared memory space, $DP \leq |S|$ processors to solve the dual problem in Eq. (18) and PP processors to recover complete solutions to the SUC problem in Eqs. (10)–(17). Interactions between different processors are presented in **Figure 1**.

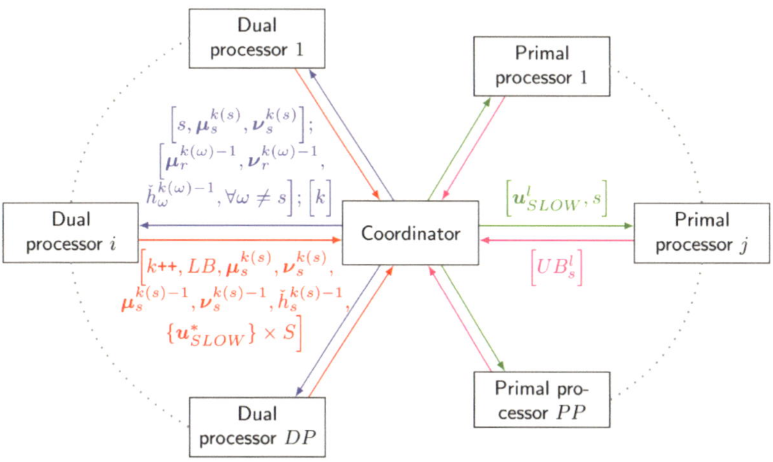

Figure 1 Asynchronous algorithm layout. Information within square brackets is read or written at a single step of the algorithm.

We maximize the dual function in Eq. (18) using a block coordinate descent (BCD) method, in which each update is performed over a block of dual variables associated with a scenario, (μ_s, ν_s) for certain $s \in S$, following the direction of the subgradient of the dual function in the block of variables (μ_s, ν_s). The BCD method is implemented in parallel and asynchronously by having each dual processor perform updates on the dual variables associated with a certain scenario, which are not being updated by any other dual processor at the same time. Scenarios whose dual variables are not currently being updated by any processor are held in the dual queue Q^D, to be updated later.

We maintain shared memory registers of Q^D. We denote the current multipliers as $\left(\mu_s^{k(s)}, \nu_s^{k(s)}\right)$ $\forall s \in S$, where $k(s)$ is the number of updates to the block of scenario s; the previous-to-current dual multipliers as $\left(\mu_s^{k(s)-1}, \nu_s^{k(s)-1}\right)$ and their associated lower bound on $h_s\left(\mu_s^{k(s)-1}, \nu_s^{k(s)-1}\right)$ as $\check{h}_s^{k(s)-1}$, $\forall s \in S$; the global update count as k; and the best lower bound found in Eqs. (10)–(17) as LB. Additionally, a shared memory register of the primal queue Q^P is required for recovering primal solutions. Then, each dual processor performs the following operations:

1. Read and remove the first scenario s from Q^D.

2. Read $\left(\mu_s^{k(s)}, \nu_s^{k(s)}\right)$ and evaluate $h_s\left(\mu_s^{k(s)}, \nu_s^{k(s)}\right)$ approximately.

3. Read $\left(\mu_\omega^{k(\omega)-1}, \nu_\omega^{k(\omega)-1}\right)$ and $\check{h}_\omega^{k(\omega)-1}$ for all $\omega \in S \setminus \{s\}$.

4. Construct the delayed multiplier vectors,

$$\bar{\mu} := \left(\mu_{s_1}^{k(s_1)-1}, \ldots, \mu_s^{k(s)}, \ldots, \mu_{s_M}^{k(s_M)-1}\right)$$
$$\bar{\nu} := \left(\nu_{s_1}^{k(s_1)-1}, \ldots, \nu_s^{k(s)}, \ldots, \nu_{s_M}^{k(s_M)-1}\right),$$

and evaluate $h_0(\bar{\mu}, \bar{\nu})$ approximately.

5. Read the current global iteration count k and perform a BCD update on the dual multipliers

$$\mu_s^{k(s)+1} := \mu_s^{k(s)} + \frac{\alpha_k}{\beta_s} \cdot \pi_s(u_{SLOW}^* - w^*)$$

$$\nu_s^{k(s)+1} := \nu_s^{k(s)} + \frac{\alpha_k}{\beta_s} \cdot \pi_s(v_{SLOW}^* - z^*),$$

where (w^*, z^*) is an approximate minimizer of Eq. (19) for $(\bar{\mu}, \bar{\nu})$, (p^*, u^*, v^*, f^*) is an approximate minimizer of Eq. (20) for $\left(\mu_s^{k(s)}, \nu_s^{k(s)}\right)$ and (u_{SLOW}^*, v_{SLOW}^*) corresponds to the commitment and startup for slow generators in (p^*, u^*, v^*, f^*).

6. Compute a new lower bound as

$$LB^{\text{new}} := \check{h}_0(\overline{\boldsymbol{\mu}}, \overline{\boldsymbol{\nu}}) + \check{h}_s\left(\boldsymbol{\mu}_s^{k(s)}, \boldsymbol{\nu}_s^{k(s)}\right) + \sum_{\omega \in S \setminus \{s\}} \check{h}_\omega^{k(\omega)-1},$$

where $\check{h}_0(\overline{\boldsymbol{\mu}}, \overline{\boldsymbol{\nu}}) \leq h_0(\overline{\boldsymbol{\mu}}, \overline{\boldsymbol{\nu}})$ and $\check{h}_s\left(\boldsymbol{\mu}_s^{k(s)}, \boldsymbol{\nu}_s^{k(s)}\right) \leq h_s\left(\boldsymbol{\mu}_s^{k(s)}, \boldsymbol{\nu}_s^{k(s)}\right)$ are the lower bounds of the MILP solution of Eqs. (19) and (20).

7. Let $k(s) := k(s) + 1$ and update in memory:

   a. $k+ = 1$.

   b. $LB := \max\{LB, LB^{\text{new}}\}$.

   c. $\left(\boldsymbol{\mu}_s^{k(s)}, \boldsymbol{\nu}_s^{k(s)}\right)$

   d. $\left(\boldsymbol{\mu}_s^{k(s)-1}, \boldsymbol{\nu}_s^{k(s)-1}\right)$ and $\check{h}_s^{k(s)-1} := \check{h}_s\left(\boldsymbol{\mu}_s^{k(s)-1}, \boldsymbol{\nu}_s^{k(s)-1}\right)$

   e. Add $\{\boldsymbol{u}_{SLOW}^*\} \times S$ to the end of Q^P.

8. Add s at the end of Q^D and return to 1.

Steps 1–3 of the dual processor algorithm are self-explanatory. Step 4 constructs a compound of the previous iterates which is useful for computing lower bounds.

During the execution of the algorithm, step 5 will perform updates to the blocks of dual variables associated to all scenarios. As $h_s(\boldsymbol{\mu}_s, \boldsymbol{\nu}_s)$ is easier to evaluate for certain scenarios than others, the blocks of dual variables associated to easier scenarios will be updated more frequently than harder scenarios. We model this process, in a simplified fashion, as if every update is performed on a randomly selected scenario from a nonuniform distribution, where the probability of selecting scenario s corresponds to

$$\beta_s := \frac{T_s^{\text{between}}}{\sum_{\omega \in S} T_\omega^{\text{between}}},$$

where T_s^{between} is the average time between two updates on scenario s ($T_s^{between}$ is estimated during execution). The asynchronous BCD method can then be understood as a stochastic approximate subgradient method [26, 27]. This is an approximate method for three reasons: (i) as the objective function contains a nonseparable nondifferentiable function $h_0(\boldsymbol{\mu}, \boldsymbol{\nu})$, there is no guarantee that the expected update direction coincides with a subgradient of the objective of Eq. (8) at the current iterate, (ii) $h_0(\boldsymbol{\mu}, \boldsymbol{\nu})$ is evaluated for a delayed version of the multipliers $(\overline{\boldsymbol{\mu}}, \overline{\boldsymbol{\nu}})$, and (iii) $h_0(\boldsymbol{\mu}, \boldsymbol{\nu})$ and $h_s(\boldsymbol{\mu}_s, \boldsymbol{\nu}_s)$ are evaluated only approximately up to a certain MILP gap. Provided that we use a diminishing, nonsummable and square-summable stepsize α_k of the type $1/k^q$, and that the error in the subgradient is bounded, the method will converge to an approximate solution of the dual problem in Eq. (8) [26, 27].

In step 6, we compute a lower bound on the primal problem Eqs. (10)–(17) using previous evaluations of $h_s(\mu_s, \nu_s)$ recorded in memory, as proposed in Ref. [6]. Step 7 updates the shared memory registers for future iterations and step 8 closes the internal loop of the dual processor.

We recover primal solutions by taking advantage of the fact that (u^*_{SLOW}, v^*_{SLOW}) is a feasible solution for (w, z) in Eqs. (10)–(17). Therefore, in order to compute complete primal solutions and obtain upper bounds for problem in Eqs. (10)–(17), we can fix $w := u^*_{SLOW}$ and $z := v^*_{SLOW}$ and solve the remaining problem, as proposed in Ref. [28]. After fixing (w, z), the remaining problem becomes separable by scenario; hence, in order to solve it, we need to solve a restricted DUC for each scenario in S. These primal evaluation jobs, i.e., solving the restricted DUC for $\{u^*_{SLOW}\} \times S$, are appended at the end of the primal queue Q^P by dual processors after each update (step 7.e). Note that we do not require storing v^*_{SLOW} because its value is implied by u^*_{SLOW}.

The primal queue is managed by the coordinator process, which assigns primal jobs to primal processors as they become available. The computation of primal solutions is therefore also asynchronous, in the sense that it runs independently of dual iterations and that the evaluation of candidate solutions u^*_{SLOW} does not require that the previous candidates have already been evaluated for all scenarios. Once a certain candidate u^l has been evaluated for all scenarios, the coordinator can compute a new upper bound to Eqs. (10)–(17) as

$$UB := \min\left\{UB, \sum_{s \in S} UB^l_s\right\}, \tag{25}$$

where UB^l_s is the upper bound associated with u^l on the restricted DUC problem of scenario s. The coordinator process keeps track of the candidate associated with the smaller upper bound throughout the execution.

Finally, the coordinator process will terminate the algorithm when $1 - LB/UB \leq \epsilon$, where ϵ is a prescribed tolerance, or when reaching a prescribed maximum solution time. At this point, the algorithm retrieves the best-found solution and the bound on the distance of this solution from the optimal objective function value.

3.3. Dual algorithm initialization

The lower bounds computed by the algorithm presented in the previous section depend on previous evaluations of $h_s(\mu_s, \nu_s)$ for other scenarios. As the evaluation of $h_s(\mu_s, \nu_s)$ can require a substantial amount of time for certain scenarios, the computation of the first lower bound considering nontrivial values of $h_s(\mu_s, \nu_s)$ for all scenarios can be delayed significantly with respect to the advance of dual iterations and primal recovery. In other words, it might be the case that the algorithm finds a very good primal solution but it is unable to terminate because it is missing the value of $h_s(\mu_s, \nu_s)$ for a single scenario.

In order to prevent these situations and in order to obtain nontrivial bounds faster, in the first pass of the dual processors over all scenarios, we can replace $h_s(\mu_s, \nu_s)$ with a surrogate $\eta_s(\mu_s, \nu_s)$ which is easier to compute, such that $\eta_s(\mu_s, \nu_s) \leq h_s(\mu_s, \nu_s)$ for any (μ_s, ν_s). We propose two alternatives for $\eta_s(\mu_s, \nu_s)$:

http://dx.doi.org/10.5772/67791

1. The linear relaxation of the scenario DUC (LP):

$$\eta_s(\boldsymbol{\mu}_s, \boldsymbol{\nu}_s) := \pi_s \inf_{p,u,v,f} \left\{ \begin{array}{c} \sum_{g \in G} \sum_{t \in T_{15}} C_g(p_{g,t}) + \sum_{g \in G \setminus G_{SLOW}} \sum_{\tau \in T_{60}} (K_g u_{g,\tau} + S_g v_{g,\tau}) + \\ \sum_{g \in G_{SLOW}} \sum_{\tau \in T_{60}} \left((K_g + \boldsymbol{\mu}_{g,s,\tau}) u_{g,\tau} + (S_g + \boldsymbol{\nu}_{g,s,\tau}) v_{g,\tau} \right) : \\ \text{linear relaxation of } (11s) - (15s) \end{array} \right\}$$

2. An optimal power flow for each period (OPF):

$$\eta_s(\boldsymbol{\mu}_s, \boldsymbol{\nu}_s) := \pi_s \sum_{t \in T_{15}} \inf_{p,u,v,f} \left\{ \begin{array}{c} \sum_{g \in G} C_g(p_g) + \frac{1}{4} \sum_{g \in G \setminus G_{SLOW}} K_g u_g + \\ \frac{1}{4} \sum_{g \in G_{SLOW}} \left(\left(K_g + \boldsymbol{\mu}_{g,s,\tau(t)}\right) u_g + \left(S_g + \boldsymbol{\nu}_{g,s,\tau(t)}\right) v_g \right) : \\ (11st) - (13st), \boldsymbol{u} \in \{0,1\}^{|G|}, \boldsymbol{v} \in \{0,1\}^{|G_{SLOW}|} \end{array} \right\},$$

where $(11st) - (13st)$ correspond to constraints Eqs. (11)–(13) for scenario s and period t.

The LP approach requires solving a linear program of the same size as the original problem in Eq. (20), but it has the advantage that it can be obtained as an intermediate result while evaluating $h_s(\boldsymbol{\mu}_s, \boldsymbol{\nu}_s)$ (the LP approach does not add extra computations to the algorithm). The OPF approach, on the other hand, requires solving many small MILP problems, which can be solved faster than the linear relaxation of Eq. (20). The OPF approach ignores several constraints and cost components, such as the startup cost of nonslow generators, and it adds extra computations to the algorithm.

3.4. Implementation and numerical experiments

We implement the DUCR model using Mosel and solve it directly using Xpress. We also implement the proposed asynchronous algorithm for SUC (described in the previous subsections) in Mosel, using the module *mmjobs* for handling parallel processes and communications, while solving the subproblems with Xpress [29]. We configure Xpress to solve the root node using the barrier algorithm and we set the termination gap to 1%, for both the DUCR and SUC subproblems, and the maximum solution wall time to 10 hours. Numerical experiments were run on the Sierra cluster hosted at the Lawrence Livermore National Laboratory. Each node of the Sierra cluster is equipped with two Intel XeonEP X5660 processors (12 cores per node) and 24GB of RAM memory. We use 10 nodes for the proposed distributed algorithm, assigning 5 nodes to dual processors, with 6 dual processors per node ($DP = 30$), and 5 nodes to primal recovery, with 12 primal processors per node. The coordinator is implemented on a primal node and occupies one primal processor ($PP = 59$).

We test the proposed algorithm on a detailed model of the Central Western European system, consisting of 656 thermal generators, 679 nodes, and 1037 lines. The model was constructed by using the network model of Hutcheon and Bialek [30], technical generator information provided to the authors by ENGIE, and multiarea demand and renewable energy information collected from national system operators (see [31] for details). We consider eight representative day types, one weekday and one weekend day per season, as being representative of the different conditions faced by the system throughout the year.

We consider 4 day-ahead scheduling models: the DUCR model and the SUC model with 30 (*SUC30*), 60 (*SUC60*), and 120 (*SUC120*) scenarios. The sizes of the different day-ahead scheduling models are presented in **Table 1**, where the size of the stochastic models refers to the size of the extensive form. While the DUCR model is of the scale of problems that fit in the memory of a single machine and can be solved by a commercial solver, the SUC models in extensive form are beyond current capabilities of commercial solvers.

Table 2 presents the solution time statistics for all day-ahead scheduling policies. In the case of SUC, we report these results for the two dual initialization alternatives proposed in Section 3.2.

The results of **Table 2** indicate that the OPF initialization significantly outperforms the LP approach in terms of termination time. This is mainly due to the fact that the OPF approach provides nontrivial lower bounds including information for all scenarios much faster than the LP approach. On the other hand, the solution times of SUC60 and DUCR indicate that, using distributed computing, we can solve SUC at a comparable run time to that required by commercial solvers for DUCR on large-scale systems. Moreover, as shown in **Table 3**, for a given hard constraint on solution wall time such as 2 h (which is common for day-ahead power system operations), the proposed distributed algorithm provides solutions to SUC with up to 60 scenarios within 2% of optimality, which is acceptable for operational purposes.

Model	Scenarios	Variables	Constraints	Integers
DUCR	1	570.432	655.784	9.552
SUC30	30	13334.400	16182.180	293.088
SUC60	60	26668.800	32364.360	579.648
SUC120	120	53337.600	64728.720	1152.768

Table 1. Problem sizes.

Model	Nodes used	Initialization	Running time [h] avg. (min.–max.)	Worst final gap [%]
DUCR	1	–	1.9 (0.6–4.2)	0.95
SUC30	10	LP	1.1 (0.7–2.2)	0.93
	10	OPF	0.8 (0.3–1.8)	1.00
SUC60	10	LP	3.2 (1.1–8.4)	1.00
	10	OPF	1.5 (0.6–4.7)	0.97
SUC120	10	LP	>6.1 (1.6–10.0)	1.68
	10	OPF	>3.0 (0.6–10.0)	1.07

Table 2. Solution time statistics over 8 day types.

http://dx.doi.org/10.5772/67791

Model	Initialization	Worst gap [%]			
		1 h	2 h	4 h	8 h
SUC30	LP	7.59	1.02	0.93	
	OPF	1.90	1.00		
SUC60	LP	23.00	5.32	5.22	4.50
	OPF	4.60	1.57	1.03	0.97
SUC120	LP	70.39	31.66	4.61	1.87
	OPF	46.69	27.00	1.42	1.07

Table 3. Worst optimality gap (over 8 day types) vs. solution wall time.

4. Scalable control for distributed energy resources

4.1. Overview

Residential demand response has gained significant attention in recent years as an underutilized source of flexibility in power systems, and is expected to become highly valuable as a balancing resource as increasing amounts of renewable energy are being integrated into the grid. However, the mobilization of demand response by means of real-time pricing, which represents the economists' gold standard and can be traced back to the seminal work of Schweppe et al. [32], has so far fallen short of expectations due to several obstacles, including regulation issues, market structure, incentives to consumers, and technological limitations.

The ColorPower architecture [7, 8, 9] aims at releasing the potent power of demand response by approaching electricity as a service of differentiated quality, rather than a commodity that residential consumers are willing to trade in real time [33]. In this architecture, the coordination problem of determining which devices should consume power at what times is solved through distributed aggregation and stochastic control. The consumer designates devices or device modes using priority tiers (colors). These tiers correspond to "service level" plans, which are easy to design and implement: we can simply map the "color" designations of electrical devices into plans. A "more flexible" color means less certainty of when a device will run (e.g., time when a pool pump runs), or lower quality service delivered by a device (e.g., wider temperature ranges, slower electrical vehicle charging). These types of economic decision-making are eminently compatible with consumer desires and economic design, as evidenced by the wide range of quality-of-service contracts offered in other industries.

Furthermore, the self-identified priority tiers of the ColorPower approach enable retail power participation in wholesale energy markets, lifting the economic obstacles for demand response: since the demand for power can be differentiated into tiers with a priority order, the demand in each tier can be separately bid into the current wholesale or local (DSO level) energy markets. The price for each tier can be set according to the cost of supplying demand response from that tier, which in turn is linked to the incentives necessary for securing customer participation in the demand response program. This allows aggregated demand to send price signals in the form of a decreasing buy bid curve. Market information thus flows bidirectionally. A small amount of flexible demand can then buffer the volatility of the overall power demand by yielding power to the inflexible devices as necessary (based upon the priority chosen by the customer), while fairly distributing power to all customer devices within a demand tier.

Technological limitations to the massive deployment of demand response are dealt with by deploying field-proven stochastic control techniques across the distribution network, with the objective of subtly shifting the schedules of millions of devices in real time, based upon the conditions of the grid. These control techniques include the CSMA/CD algorithms that permit cellular phones to share narrow radio frequency bands, telephone switch control algorithms, and operating system thread scheduling, as well as examples from nature such as social insect hive behaviors and bacterial quorum sensing. Moreover, the ubiquity of Internet communications allows us to consider using the Internet platform itself for end-to-end communications between machines.

At a high level, the ColorPower algorithm operates by aggregating the demand flexibility state information of each agent into a global estimate of total consumer flexibility. This aggregate and the current demand target are then broadcast via IP multicast throughout the system, and every local controller (typically one per consumer or one per device) combines the overall model and its local state to make a stochastic control decision. With each iteration of aggregation, broadcast, and control, the overall system moves toward the target demand, set by the utility or the ISO, TSO, or DSO, allowing the system as a whole to rapidly achieve any given target of demand and closely tracking target ramps. Note that aggregation has the beneficial side-effect of preserving the privacy of individual consumers: their demand information simply becomes part of an overall statistic.

The proposed architectural approach supplements the inadequacy of pure market-based control approaches by introducing an automated, distributed, and cooperative communications feedback loop between the system and large populations of cooperative devices at the edge of the network. TSO markets and the evolving DSO local energy markets of the future will have both deep markets and distributed control architecture pushed out to the edge of the network. This smart grid architecture for demand response in the mass market is expected to be a key asset in addressing the challenges of renewable energy integration and the transition to a low-carbon economy.

4.2. The ColorPower control problem

A ColorPower system consists of a set of n agents, each owning a set of electrical devices organized into k colors, where lower-numbered colors are intended to be shut off first (e.g., 1 for "green" pool pumps, 2 for "green" HVAC, 3 for "yellow" pool pumps, etc.), and where each color has its own time constants.

Within each color, every device is either *Enabled*, meaning that it can draw power freely, or *Disabled*, meaning that has been shut off or placed in a lower power mode. In order to prevent damage to appliances and/or customer annoyance, devices must wait through a *Refractory* period after switching between *Disabled* and *Enabled*, before they return to being *Flexible* and can switch again. These combinations give four device states (e.g., *Enabled* and *Flexible*, *EF*), through which each device in the ColorPower system moves according to the modified Markov model of **Figure 2**: randomly from *EF* to *DR* and *DF* to *ER* (becoming disabled with probability p_{off} and enabled with probability p_{on}) and by randomized timeout from *ER* to *EF* and *DR* to *DF* (a fixed length of $T_{\cdot F}$ plus a uniform random addition of up to $T_{\cdot V}$).

The ColorPower control problem can then be stated as dynamically adjusting p_{on} and p_{off} for each agent and color tier, in a distributed manner, so that the aggregate consumption of the system follows a demand goal given by the operator of the high-voltage network.

4.3. The ColorPower architecture

The block diagram of the ColorPower control architecture is presented in **Figure 3**. Each ColorPower client (i.e., the controller inside a device) regulates the state transitions of the devices under its control. Each client state $s(t,\ a)$ is aggregated to produce a global state estimate $\hat{s}(t)$, which is broadcasted along with a goal $g(t)$ (the demand target set by the utility or the ISO, TSO, or DSO), allowing clients to shape demand by independently computing the control state $c(t, a)$.

The state $s(t,\ a)$ of a client a at time t sums the power demands of the device(s) under its control, and these values are aggregated using a distributed algorithm (e.g., a spanning tree in Ref. [7]) and fed to a state estimator to get an overall estimate of the true state $\hat{s}(t)$ of total demand in each state for each color. This estimate is then broadcast to all clients (e.g., by gossip-like diffusion in Ref. [7]), along with the demand shaping goal $g(t)$ for the next total *Enabled* demand over all colors. The controller at each client a sets its control state $c(t, a)$, defined as the set of transition probabilities $p_{\text{on}, i, a}$ and $p_{\text{off}, i, a}$ for each color i. Finally, demands move through their states according to those transition probabilities, subject to exogenous disturbances such as changes in demand due to customer override, changing environmental conditions, imprecision in measurement, among others.

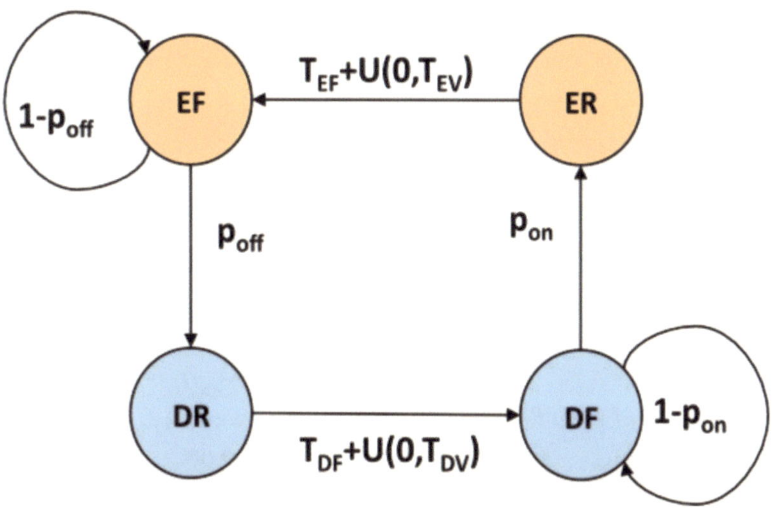

Figure 2 Markov model-based device state switching [8, 9].

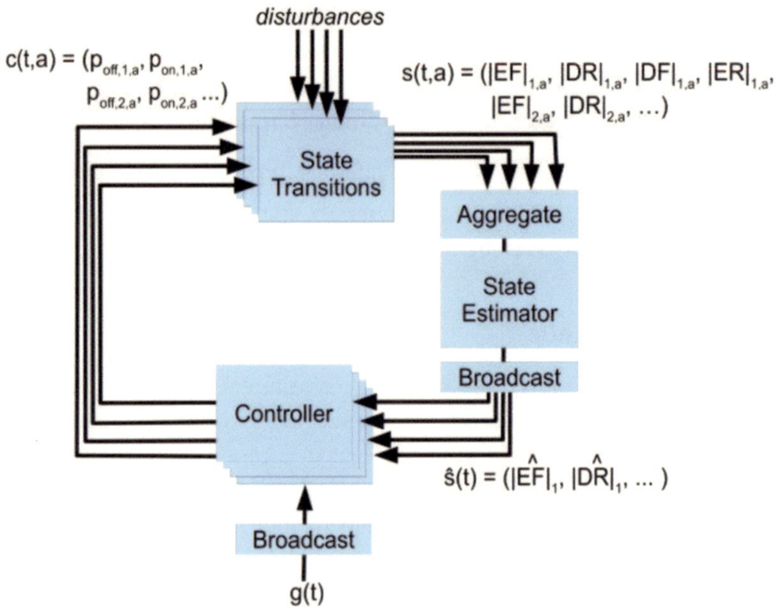

Figure 3 Block diagram of the control architecture [8, 9].

Note that the aggregation and broadcast algorithms must be chosen carefully in order to ensure that the communication requirements are lightweight enough to allow control rounds that last for a few seconds on low-cost hardware. The choice of algorithm depends on the network structure: for mesh networks, for example, spanning tree aggregation and gossip-based broadcast are fast and efficient (for details, see [7]).

4.4. ColorPower control algorithm

The ColorPower control algorithm, determines the control vector $c(t, a)$ by a stochastic controller formulated to satisfy four constraints:

Goal tracking: The total *Enabled* demand in $s(t)$ should track $g(t)$ as closely as possible: i.e., the sum of *Enabled* demand over all colors *i* should be equal to the goal. This is formalized as the equation:

$$g(t) = \sum_i (|EF_i| + |ER_i|).$$

Color priority: Devices with lower-numbered colors should be shut off before devices with higher-numbered colors. This is formalized as:

$$|EF_i| + |ER_i| = \begin{cases} D_i - D_{i+1} & \text{if } D_i \leq g(t) \\ g(t) - D_{i+1} & \text{if } D_{i+1} \leq g(t) < D_i \\ 0 & \text{otherwise,} \end{cases}$$

so that devices are *Enabled* from the highest color downward, where D_i is the demand for the *i*th color and above:

http://dx.doi.org/10.5772/67791

$$D_{\mathrm{i}} = \sum_{j \geq i} (|EF_j| + |ER_j| + |DF_j| + |DR_j|).$$

Fairness: When the goal leads to some devices with a particular color being *Enabled* and other devices with that color being *Disabled*, each device has the same expected likelihood of being *Disabled*. This means that the control state is identical for every client.

Cycling: Devices within a color trade-off which devices are *Enabled* and which are *Disabled* such that no device is unfairly burdened by initial bad luck. This is ensured by asserting the constraint:

$$(|EF_i| > 0) \cap (|DF_i| > 0) \Rightarrow (p_{\mathrm{on},\, i,\, a} > 0) \cap (p_{\mathrm{off},\, i,\, a} > 0).$$

This means that any color with a mixture of *Enabled* and *Disabled Flexible* devices will always be switching the state of some devices. For this last constraint, there is a tradeoff between how quickly devices cycle and how much flexibility is held in reserve for future goal tracking; we balance these with a target ratio f of the minimum ratio between pairs of corresponding *Flexible* and *Refractory* states.

Since the controller acts indirectly, by manipulating the p_{on} and p_{off} transition probabilities of devices, the only resource available for meeting these constraints is the demand in the flexible states *EF* and *DF* for each tier. When it is not possible to satisfy all four constraints simultaneously, the ColorPower controller prioritizes the constraints in order of their importance. Fairness and qualitative color guarantees are given highest priority, since these are part of the contract with customers: fairness by ensuring that the expected enablement fraction of each device is equivalent (though particular clients may achieve this in different ways, depending on their type and customer settings). Qualitative priority is handled by rules that prohibit flexibility from being considered by the controller outside of contractually allowable circumstances. Constraints are enforced sequentially. First comes goal tracking—the actual shaping of demand to meet power schedules. Second is the soft color priority, which ensures that in those transient situations when goal tracking causes some devices to be in the wrong state, it is eventually corrected. Cycling is last, because it is defined only over long periods of time and thus is the least time critical to satisfy. A controller respecting the aforementioned constraints is described in Ref. [8].

4.5. Numerical experiment

We have implemented and tested the proposed demand response approach into the ColorPower software platform [8]. Simulations are executed with the following parameters: 10 trials per condition for 10,000 controllable devices, each device consumes 1 kW of power (for a total of 10 MW demand), devices are 20% green (low priority), 50% yellow (medium priority) and 30% red (high priority), the measurement error is $\varepsilon = 0.1\%$ (0.001), the rounds are 10 seconds long and all the *Refractory* time variables are 40 rounds. Error is measured by taking the ratio of the difference of a state from optimal versus the total power.

The results of the simulation test are shown in **Figure 4**. When peak control is desired, the aggregate demand remains below the quota, while individual loads are subjected stochastically

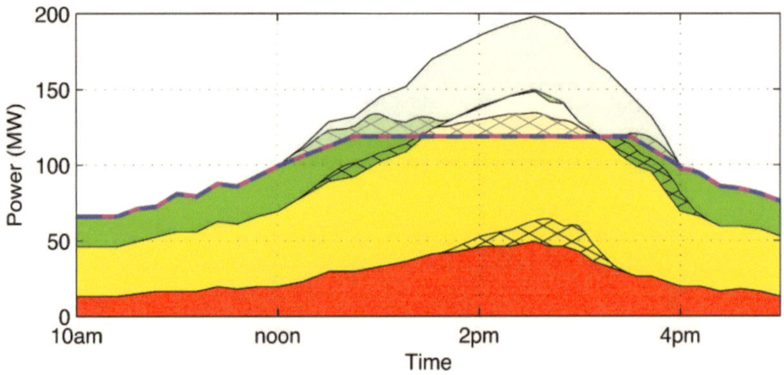

Figure 4 Simulation results with 10,000 independently fluctuating power loads. Demand is shown as a stacked graph, with enabled demand at the bottom in dark tones, disabled demand at the top in light tones, and Refractory demand cross hatched. The goal is the dashed line, which coincides with the total enabled demand for the experiment. The plot illustrates a peak shaving case where a power quota, the demand response target that may be provided from an externally-generated demand forecast, is used as a guide for the demand to follow.

to brief curtailments. Post-event rush-in, a potentially severe problem for both traditional demand response and price signal-based control systems, is also managed gracefully due to the specific design of the modified Markov model of **Figure 2**.

Taken together, these results indicate that the ColorPower approach, when coupled with an appropriate controller, should have the technological capability to flexibly and resiliently shape demand in most practical deployment scenarios.

5. Conclusions

We present two applications of distributed computing in power systems. On the one hand, we optimize high-voltage power system operations using a distributed asynchronous algorithm capable of solving stochastic unit commitment in comparable run times to those of a deterministic unit commitment model with reserve requirements, and within operationally acceptable time frames. On the other hand, we control demand response at the distribution level using stochastic distributed control, thereby enabling large-scale demand shaping during real-time operations of power systems. Together, both applications of distributed computing demonstrate the potential for efficiently managing flexible resources in smart grids and for systematically coping with the uncertainty and variability introduced by renewable energy.

Acknowledgements

The authors acknowledge the Fair Isaac Corporation FICO for providing licenses for Xpress, and the Lawrence Livermore National Laboratory for granting access and computing time at the Sierra cluster. This research was funded by the ENGIE Chair on Energy Economics and Energy Risk Management and by the Université catholique de Louvain through an FSR grant.

http://dx.doi.org/10.5772/67791

Nomenclature

Deterministic and stochastic unit commitment

Sets

T_{60}	Hourly periods, $T_{60} := \{1, \ldots, \|T_{60}\|\}$
T_{15}	15-min periods, $T_{15} := \{1, \ldots, \|T_{15}\|\}$
S	Scenarios, $S := \{s_1, \ldots, s_M\}$
A	Reserve areas
N	Buses
L	Lines
G	Thermal generators
$N(a)$	Buses in area a
$L(n, m)$	Lines between buses n and m, directed from n to m
$G(n)$	Thermal generators at bus or bus set n
G_{SLOW}	Slow generators, $G_{SLOW} \subseteq G$

Parameters

$\tau(t)$	Corresponding hour of quarter t
π_s	Probability of scenario s
$D_{n,t}$	Demand at bus n in period t
$\overline{\xi}_{n,t}, \xi_{n,s,t}$	Forecast renewable supply, bus n, scenario s, quarter t
$\mathcal{R}_a^2, \mathcal{R}_a^3$	Secondary and tertiary reserve requirements in area a
$\Delta T_2, \Delta T_3$	Delivery time of secondary and tertiary reserves, $0 < \Delta T_2 < \Delta T_3 \leq 15$
$F_l^{\pm}$	Flow bounds, line l
B_l	Susceptance, line l
$n(l), m(l)$	Departing and arrival buses, line l
$P_g^{\pm}$	Minimum stable level and maximum run capacity, generator g
$R_g^{\pm}$	Maximum 15-min ramp down/up, generator g
TL_g	Maximum state transition level, generator g
UT_g, DT_g	Minimum up/down times, generator g
K_g	Hourly no-load cost, generator g
S_g	Startup cost, generator g
$C_g(p)$	Quarterly production cost function, generator g (convex, piece-wise linear)

Variables

$p_{g,t}, p_{g,s,t}$	Production, generator g, scenario t, quarter t
$f_{l,t}, f_{l,s,t}$	Flow through line l, scenario s, quarter t
$\theta_{n,t}, \theta_{n,s,t}$	Voltage angle, bus n, scenario s, quarter t
r_g^2, r_g^3	Capacity and ramp up rate reservation for secondary and tertiary reserve provision, generator g, quarter t

$u_{g,\tau}, u_{g,s,\tau}$	commitment, generator g, scenario s, hour τ
$v_{g,\tau}, v_{g,s,\tau}$	startup, generator g, scenario s, hour τ
$w_{g,\tau}, z_{g,\tau}$	Nonanticipative commitment and startup, generator g, hour τ
$\mu_{g,s,\tau}, \nu_{g,s,\tau}$	Dual multipliers of nonanticipativity constraints, generator g, scenario s, hour τ

Asynchronous distributed algorithm for stochastic unit commitment

Sets

Q^D	Dual queue (ordered set) of scenarios
Q^P	Primal queue of pairs: ‹candidate solution, scenario›

Parameters

DP, PP	Number of dual and primal processors
α_k	Stepsize, asynchronous subgradient method
β_s	Stepsize scaling factor, scenario s

Variables

LB, UB	Lower and upper bound on objective of stochastic unit commitment
UB_s^l	Upper bound of primal candidate l on scenario s

Distributed control for demand response

Parameters

$T_{DF,i}$	Fixed rounds of disabled refractory time for tier i
$T_{DV,i}$	Maximum random rounds disabled refractory time for tier i
$T_{EF,i}$	Fixed rounds of enabled refractory time for tier i
$T_{EV,i}$	Maximum random rounds enabled refractory time for tier i
f	Target minimum ratio of flexible to refractory demand
α	Proportion of goal discrepancy corrected each round

Variables

$s(t,a)$	State of demand for agent a at time t
$s(t)$	State of total power demand (watts) at time t
$\hat{s}(t)$	Estimate of $s(t)$
$\lvert X_{i,a}\rvert$	Power demand (watts) in state X for color i at agent a
$\lvert X_i\rvert$	Total power demand (watts) in state X for color i
$\lvert\hat{X}_i\rvert$	Estimate of $\lvert X_i\rvert$
$g(t)$	Goal total enabled demand for time t
$c(t,a)$	Control state for agent a at time t
$p_{\text{off},i,a}$	Probability of a flexible color i device disabling at agent a
$p_{\text{on},i,a}$	Probability of a flexible color i device enable at agent a
D_i	Demand for ith color and above

http://dx.doi.org/10.5772/67791

Author details

Ignacio Aravena[1]*, Anthony Papavasiliou[1] and Alex Papalexopoulos[2]

*Address all correspondence to: ignacio.aravena@uclouvain.be

1 CORE, Université Catholique de Louvain, Louvain-la-Neuve, Belgium

2 ECCO International, San Francisco, CA, USA

References

[1] X. Fang, S. Misra, G. Xue and D. Yang, "Smart grid — the new and improved power grid: a survey," in IEEE Communications Surveys & Tutorials, vol. 14, no. 4, pp. 944–980, Fourth Quarter 2012.

[2] V.C. Ramesh, "On distributed computing for on-line power system applications," International Journal of Electrical Power & Energy Systems, vol. 18, no. 8, pp. 527–533, 1996.

[3] D. Falcão, "High performance computing in power system applications," in Vector and Parallel Processing – VECPAR'96 (J. Palma and J. Dongarra, eds.), vol. 1215 of Lecture Notes in Computer Science, pp. 1-23, Springer Berlin Heidelberg, 1997.

[4] M. Shahidehpour and Y. Wang, Communication and Control in Electric Power Systems: Appications of parallel and distributed processing, Wiley-IEEE Press, Piscataway, New Jersey, USA, July 2003.

[5] S. Bera, S. Misra and J. J. P. C. Rodrigues, "Cloud computing applications for smart grid: a survey," in IEEE Transactions on Parallel and Distributed Systems, vol. 26, no. 5, pp. 1477–1494, May 2015.

[6] I. Aravena and A. Papavasiliou, "Distributed Control for Small Customer Energy Demand Management," 2015 IEEE Power & Energy Society General Meeting, Denver, CO, 2015, pp. 1–5.

[7] V. V. Ranade and J. Beal, "Distributed control for small customer energy demand management", 2010 Fourth IEEE International Conference on Self-Adaptive and Self-Organizing Systems, Budapest, 2010, pp. 11–20.

[8] J. Beal, J. Berliner and K. Hunter, "Fast precise distributed control for energy demand management," 2012 IEEE Sixth International Conference on Self-Adaptive and Self-Organizing Systems (SASO), Lyon, 2012, pp. 187–192.

[9] A. Papalexopoulos, J. Beal and S. Florek, "Precise mass-market energy demand management through stochastic distributed computing," IEEE Transactions on Smart Grid, vol. 4, no. 4, pp. 2017–2027, Dec. 2013.

[10] M. Caramanis, E. Ntakou, W. W. Hogan, A. Chakrabortty and J. Schoene, "Co-optimization of power and reserves in dynamic T&D Power markets with nondispatchable renewable generation and distributed energy resources," in Proceedings of the IEEE, vol. 104, no. 4, pp. 807–836, April 2016.

[11] APX Group, Belpex, Cegedel Net, EEX, ELIA Group, EnBw, E-On Netz, Powernext, RTE, RWE, and TenneT, "A report for the regulators of the Central West European (CWE) region on the final design of the market coupling solution in the region, by the CWE MC Project," January 2010.

[12] 50Hertz Transmission GmbH, Amprion GmbH, Elia System Operator NV, TenneT TSO B. V., TenneT TSO GmbH, and TransnetBW GmbH, "Potential cross-border balancing cooperation between the Belgian, Dutch and German electricity Transmission System Operators," October 2014.

[13] PJM Interconnection LLC, "PJM Manual 11: Energy & Ancillary Services Market Operations," Revision 86, February 1, 2017.

[14] Midcontinent ISO, "BPM 002 Energy and Operating Reserve Markets Business Practice Manual," 15 March 2016.

[15] S. Takriti, J. R. Birge, and E. Long, "A stochastic model for the unit commitment problem," IEEE Transactions on Power Systems, vol. 11, no. 3,pp. 1497–1508, Aug 1996.

[16] P. Carpentier, G. Gohen, J.-C. Culioli, and A. Renaud, "Stochastic optimization of unit commitment: a new decomposition framework," IEEE Transactions on Power Systems, vol. 11, pp. 1067–1073, May 1996.

[17] M. Tahanan, W. van Ackooij, A. Frangioni, and F. Lacalandra, "Large-scale unit commitment under uncertainty," 4OR, vol. 13, no. 2, pp. 115–171, 2015.

[18] J.P. Deane, G. Drayton, B.P. Ó Gallachóir, "The impact of sub-hourly modelling in power systems with significant levels of renewable generation," Applied Energy, vol. 113, pp. 152–158, January 2014.

[19] A. Frangioni, C. Gentile and F. Lacalandra, "Tighter approximated MILP formulations for unit commitment problems," in IEEE Transactions on Power Systems, vol. 24, no. 1, pp. 105–113, Feb. 2009.

[20] D. Rajan and S. Takriti. Minimum up/down polytopes of the unit commitment problem with start-up costs. IBM Research Report RC23628, Thomas J. Watson Research Center, June 2005.

[21] A. Papavasiliou, S. S. Oren and B. Rountree, "Applying high performance computing to transmission-constrained stochastic unit commitment for renewable energy integration," in IEEE Transactions on Power Systems, vol. 30, no. 3, pp. 1109–1120, May 2015.

[22] K. Kim and V.M. Zavala, "Algorithmic innovations and software for the dual decomposition method applied to stochastic mixed-integer programs," Optimization Online, 2015.

[23] K. Cheung, D. Gade, C. Silva-Monroy, S.M. Ryan, J.P. Watson, R.J.B. Wets, and D.L. Woodruff, "Toward scalable stochastic unit commitment. Part 2: solver configuration and performance assessment," Energy Systems, vol. 6, no. 3, pp. 417–438, 2015.

[24] R.T. Rockafellar and R.J.-B. Wets, "Scenarios and policy aggregation in optimization under uncertainty," Mathematics of Operations Research, vol. 16, no. 1, pp. 119–147, 1991.

[25] A. Nedić, D. Bertsekas, and V. Borkar, "Distributed asynchronous incremental subgradient methods," in Inherently Parallel Algorithms in Feasibility and Optimization and Their Applications (Y. Butnariu, S. Reich and Y. Censor eds.), vol. 8 of Studies in Computational Mathematics, pp. 381–407, Amsterdam: Elsevier, 2001.

[26] Yuri Ermoliev, "Stochastic quasigradient methods and their application to system optimization," Stochastics, vol. 9, no. 1–2, pp. 1–36, 1983.

[27] K. Kiwiel, "Convergence of approximate and incremental subgradient methods for convex optimization," SIAM Journal on Optimization, vol. 14, no. 3, pp. 807–840, 2004.

[28] Shabbir Ahmed, "A scenario decomposition algorithm for 0–1 stochastic programs," Operations Research Letters, vol. 41, no. 6, pp. 565–569, November 2013.

[29] Y. Colombani and S. Heipcke. Multiple models and parallel solving with Mosel, February 2014. Available at: http://community.fico.com/docs/DOC-1141.

[30] N. Hutcheon and J. W. Bialek, "Updated and validated power flow model of the main continental European transmission network," 2013 IEEE Grenoble Conference, Grenoble, 2013, pp. 1–5. doi: 10.1109/PTC.2013.6652178

[31] I. Aravena and A. Papavasiliou, "Renewable Energy Integration in Zonal Markets," in IEEE Transactions on Power Systems, vol. 32, no. 2, pp. 1334–1349, March 2017. doi: 10.1109/TPWRS.2016.2585222

[32] F. C. Schweppe, R. D. Tabors, J. L. Kirtley, H. R. Outhred, F. H. Pickel and A. J. Cox, "Homeostatic utility control," IEEE Transactions on Power Apparatus and Systems, vol. PAS-99, no. 3, pp. 1151–1163, May 1980.

[33] Shmuel S. Oren, "Product Differentiation in Service Industries". Working paper presented at the First Annual Conference on Pricing, New York, NY, December 1987.

Chapter 4

GPU Computing Taxonomy

Abdelrahman Ahmed Mohamed Osman

Additional information is available at the end of the chapter

http://dx.doi.org/10.5772/intechopen.68179

Abstract

Over the past few years, a number of efforts have been made to obtain benefits from graphic processing unit (GPU) devices by using them in parallel computing. The main advantage of GPU computing is that it provides cheap parallel processing environments for those who need to solve single program multiple data (SPMD) problems. In this chapter, a GPU computing taxonomy is proposed for classifying GPU computing into four different classes depending on different strategies of combining CPUs and GPUs.

Keywords: host, device, GPU computing, single program multiple data (SPMD)

1. Objective

The objective of this chapter is as follows:

- Divide graphic processing unit (GPU) computing into four different classes.
- How to code different classes.
- Speedup computations using GPU computing.

2. Introduction

Despite the dramatic increase in computer processing power over the past few years [1], the appetite for more processing power is still rising. The main reason is that as more power becomes available, new types of work and applications that require more power are generated. The general trend is that new technology enables new applications and opens new horizons that demand further power and the introduction of some newer technologies.

Developments at the high end of computing have been motivated by complex systems such as simulation and modelling problems, speech recognition training, climate modelling and the human genome.

However, there are indications that commercial applications will also be in demand for high processing powers. This is mainly because of the increase in the volumes of data treated by these applications [2].

There are many approaches to increase computer processing power like improving the processing power of computer processors, using multiple processors or multiple computers to perform computations or using graphics processing unit (GPU) to speed up computations.

2.1. Why we need parallel computing

There are many reasons for parallelization, like speed up execution, overcome memory capacity limit and execute application that is distributed in its nature. The main reason for parallelization is to speed up the execution of applications. Another problem that arises in the era of big data is that the huge data, which need to be processed, do not fit in a single computer memory. Some applications are distributed in their nature, where parts of an application must be located in widely dispersed sites [3].

2.2. Important terminology

There are many important terminologies that help in understanding parallelization, here in this section we will talk about some of them.

2.2.1. Load balancing

The load balancing is an important issue for performance. It is a way of keeping all the processors busy as much as possible. This issue arises constantly in any discussion of parallel processing [3].

2.2.2. Latency, throughput and bandwidth

Latency, throughput and bandwidth are important factors that affect the performance of computations. Here is a brief definition for them.

- Communication latency is the time for one bit to travel from source to destination, e.g. from a CPU to GPU or from one host/device to another.
- Processor latency can be defined as the time to finish one task. While throughput can be defined as the rate at which we complete a large number of tasks (a number of tasks done in a given amount of time).
- Bandwidth is the number of bits per unit time that can be travelling in parallel. This can be affected by factors such as the bus width in a memory or the number of parallel network paths in a cluster and also by the speed of the links [3].

http://dx.doi.org/10.5772/intechopen.68179

2.2.3. Floating point operation (FLOP)

It is a unit for measuring performance. It is about how many floating-point calculations can be performed in 1 s. The calculations can be adding, subtracting, multiplying or dividing two floating-point numbers. For example, 3.456 + 56.897 is equal to one flop.

Units of flops are as follows:

- Megaflop = million flops.
- Gigaflop = billion flops (million megaflops).
- Teraflop= trillions flops.
- Petaflop = quadrillion.
- Exaflop = quintillion.

3. Introduction to GPU

The revolutionary progress made by GPU-based computers helps in speeding up computations and in accelerating scientific, analytics and other compute intensive codes. Due to their massively parallel architecture with thousands of smaller, efficient cores, GPU enables the completion of computationally intensive tasks much faster than conventional CPUs, because CPUs have a relatively small number of cores [4, 5].

Due to these features, GPU devices are now used in many institutions, universities, government labs and small and medium businesses around the world to solve big problems using parallelization. The acceleration of application is done by offloads the parallel portions of the application to GPU's cores, while the remainder serial code runs on the CPU's core. GPU computing can be used to accelerate many applications, such as image and signal processing, data mining, human genome, data analysis and image and video rendering [6].

Currently, many of the fastest supercomputers in the top 500 are built of thousands of GPU devices. For example, Titan achieved 17.59 Pflop/s on the Linpack benchmark using 261,632 of its NVIDIA K20x accelerator cores.

The reasons for the spread of using GPU devices in high performance computing is that it has many features such as it is massively parallel, contains hundreds of cores, is able to run thousands of threads at the same time, is cheap and anyone can use it even in laptops and personal computers and is highly available and it is programmable [7].

4. GPU architecture

GPU is a device that contains hundreds to thousands of arithmetic processing units (ALUs) with a same size. This makes GPU capable of runing thousands of threads concurrently (able to do millions of similar calculations at the same time in parallel), **Figure 1**. These threads need to be independent of each other without synchronization issues to run concurrently. Parallelism of threads in a GPU is suitable for executing the same copy of a single program on different data [single program multiple data (SPMD)], i.e. data parallelism [8].

> SPMD is different from single instruction, multiple data (SIMD). In SPMD, the same code of the program executed in parallel on different parts of data, while in SIMD, the same instruction is executed at the same time in all processing units [9].

CPUs are low latency, low throughput processors (faster for serial processing), while GPUs are high latency, high throughput processors (optimized for maximum throughput and for scalable parallel processing).

GPU architecture consists of two main components, global memory and streaming multiprocessors (SMs). The global memory is the main memory for the GPU and it is accessible by both GPU and CPU with high bandwidth. While SMs contain many simple cores that execute the parallel computations, the number of SMs in a device and the number of cores in SMs differ from one device to another. For example, Fermi has 16 SMs with 32 cores on each one (with the total cores equal to 16 × 32 = 512 cores), see **Table 1** for different GPU devices.

There are different GPU memory hierarchies for different devices. **Figure 2** shows an example of NVIDIA Fermi memory hierarchy with following memories:

- Registers.
- Shared memory and L1 cache (primary cache).
- Constant memory.
- Texture memory and read-only cache.
- L2 cache (secondary cache).
- Global (main) memory and local memory.

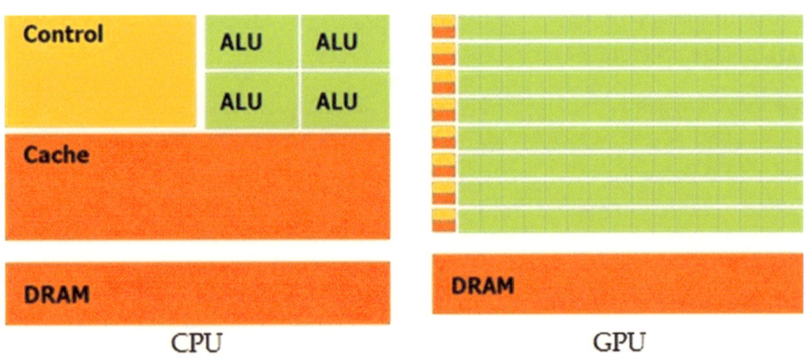

Figure 1. CPU vs. GPU, from Ref. [8].

http://dx.doi.org/10.5772/intechopen.68179

	GTX 480	GTX 580	GTX 680
Architecture	GF100	GF110	GK104
SM/SMX	15	16	8
CUDA cores	480	512	1536
Core frequency	700 MHz	772 MHz	1006 MHz
Compute power	1345 GFLOPS	1581 GFLOPS	3090 GFLOPS
Memory BW	177.4 GB/s	192.2 GB/s	192.2 GB/s
Transistors	3.2B	3.0B	3.5B
Technology	40 nm	40 nm	28 nm
Power	250 W	244 W	195 W

Table 1. Comparisons between NVIDIA GPU architecture, from Ref. [10].

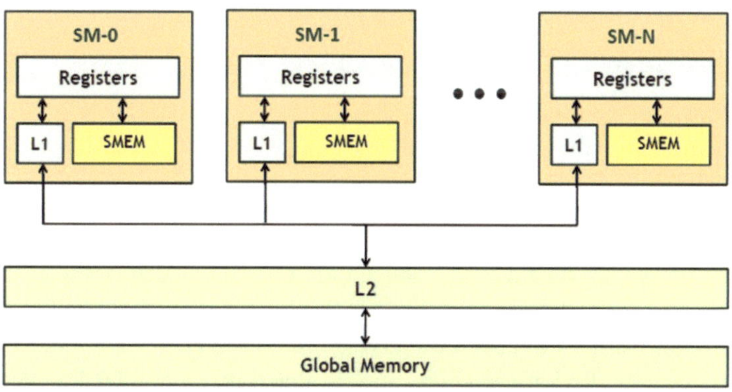

Figure 2. NVIDIA Fermi memory hierarchy, from Ref. [11].

5. GPU taxonomy

GPU computing can be divided into four different classes according to the different combinations between hosts and devices, **Figure 3**. These classes are as follows:

(1) Single host with single device (SHSD).

(2) Single host with multiple devices (SHMD).

(3) Multiple hosts with single device in each (MHSD).

(4) Multiple hosts with multiple devices (MHMD).

In the rest of this section, we will talk about each class separately.

	Single Device	Multiple Device
Single Host	SHSD	SHMD
Multiple Host	MHSD	MHMD

Figure 3. GPU computing taxonomy.

5.1. Single host, single device (SHSD)

The first class (type) in GPU taxonomy is the single host with single device (SHSD), as shown in **Figure 4**. It is composed of one host (computer) with one GPU device installed in it. Normally, the host will run the codes that are similar to conventional programming that we know (may be serial), while the parallel part of the code will be executed in the device's cores concurrently (massive parallelism).

The processing flow of SHSD computing includes:

- Transfer input data from CPU's memory to GPU's memory.
- Load GPU program and execute it.
- Transfer results from GPU's memory to CPU's memory [12].

The example of SHSD is shown in **Figure 5**; data transferred from CPU host to GPU device are coming through a communication bus connecting GPU to CPU. This communication bus is of type PCI-express with data transfer rate equal to 8 GB/s, which is the weakest link in the connection (new fast generation is available, see Section 6.1 for more details). The other links in the figure are the memory bandwidth between main memory DDR3 and CPU (42 GB/s), and the memory bandwidth between GPU and its global memory GDDR5 (288 GB/s).

Bandwidth limited

> Because transfer data between the CPU and GPU is expensive, we will always try to minimize the data transfer between the CPU and GPU. Therefore, if processors request data at too high a rate, the memory system cannot keep up. No amount of latency hiding helps this. Overcoming bandwidth limits are a common challenge for GPU-compute application developers [14].

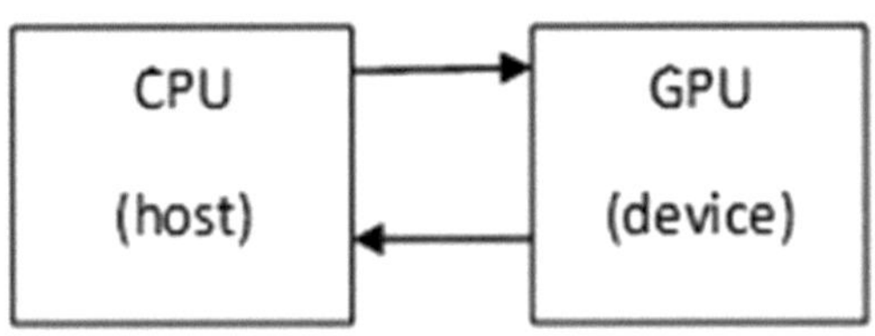

Figure 4. Single host, single device (SHSD).

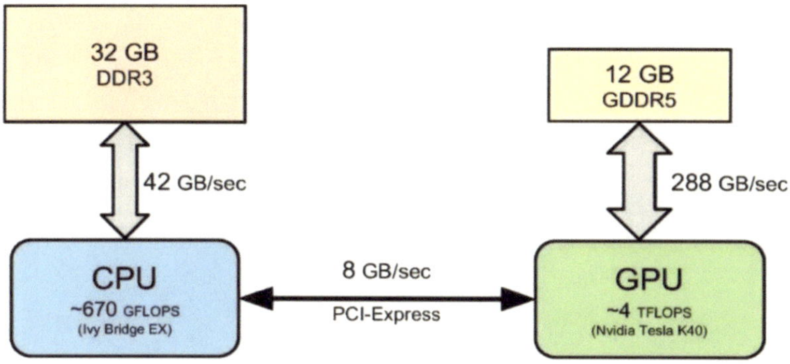

Figure 5. Example of SHSD class, from Ref. [13].

5.2. Single host, multiple device (SHMD)

In this section, we can use single host with multiple devices installed in it (SHMD), **Figures 6** and **7**. SHMD can be used to run parallel tasks in installed GPUs, with each GPU run sub-tasks in in their cores.

We can use a notation like SHMD (d, to show the number of devices that installed in the host. For example, if we have a single host with three GPU devices installed in it, we can write this as SHMD (3).

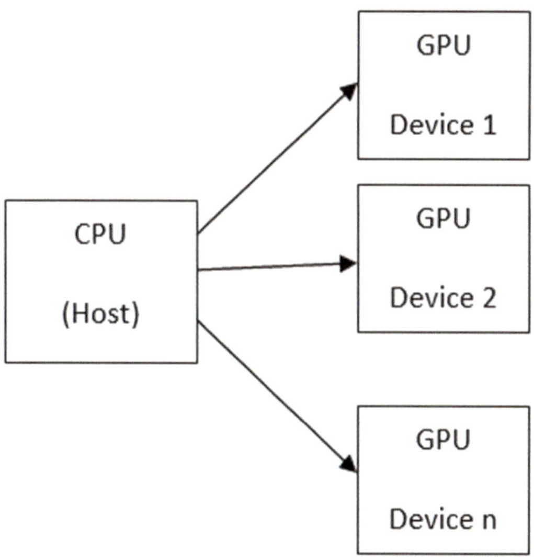

Figure 6. Single host, multiple device [SHMD (n)].

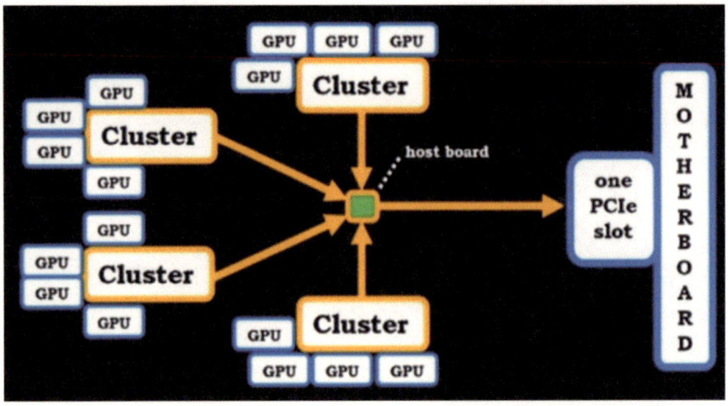

Figure 7. Server of type SHMD (16). Image from: https://www.youtube.com/watch?v=Vm9mFtSq2sg.

5.3. Multiple host, single device (MHSD)

Multiple host with single device in each host (MHSD) is an architecture for using a GPU cluster connecting many SHSD nodes together, **Figure 8**.

We can use the notation MHSD (h) to define the number of hosts in this architecture. For example, the architecture in **Figure 7** is an MHSD (4), where four nodes (SHSD) are connected in a network.

5.4. Multiple host, multiple device (MHMD)

Multiple host with multiple devices in each host (MHMD) is a GPU cluster with a number of SHMD nodes (where all nodes may have the same number of devices or may have a different number of devices), **Figure 9**.

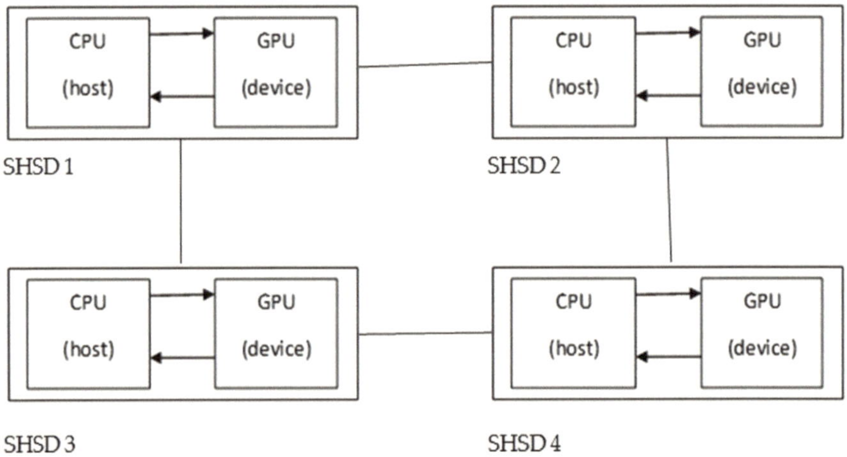

Figure 8. MHSD (4).

http://dx.doi.org/10.5772/intechopen.68179

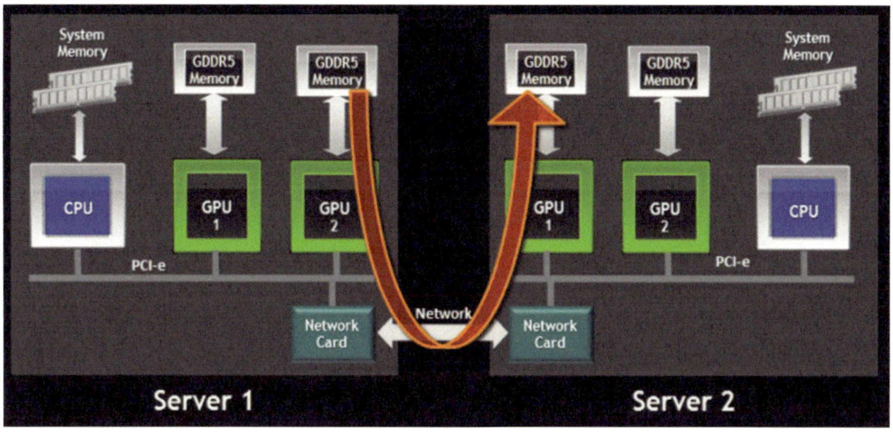

Figure 9. GPU cluster [MHMD (2,2)], image from: http://timdettmers.com/2014/09/21/how-to-build-and-use-a-multi-gpu-system-for-deep-learning.

We can use MHMD (h, d) notation to denote the number of hosts and the number of devices in each host, where h is for the number of hosts and d is for the number of devices. If the number of devices in each node is not equal, we can ignore the second parameter by putting x as do not care, MHMD (h, x).

6. Communications

There are two types of connections that can be used in GPU computing:

(1) The connection between the GPU devices and host (in SHSD and SHMD).

(2) The connection between different hosts (in MHSD and MDMD).

In this section, we will discuss about each one below.

6.1. Peripheral component interconnect express (PCIe)

PCIe is a standard point-to-point connection used to connect internal devices in a computer (used to connect two or more PCIe devices). For example, you can connect GPU to CPU or other GPU, or connect network card like InfiniBand with CPU or GPU, because most of these devices now are PCIe devices.

PCIe started in 1992 with 133 MB/s and increased to reach 533 MB/s in 1995. Then in 1995, PCIX appeared with a transfer rate of 1066 MB/s (1 GB/s). In 2004, PCIe generation 1.x came with 2.5 GB/s and then generation 2.x in 2007 with 5 GB/s, after that generation 3.x appeared in 2011 with a transfer rate equal to 8 GB/s and the latest generation 4.x in 2016 came with a transfer rate reaching 16 GB/s [15–17].

PCIe is doubling the data rate in each new generation.

6.2. Communication between nodes

In GPU cluster (MHSD or MHMD), the main bottleneck is the communications between nodes (network bandwidth) that is how much data can be transferred from computer to computer per second.

If we use none direct data transfer between different nodes in GPU cluster, then the data transferred in the following steps:

- GPU in node 1 to CPU in node 1.
- CPU in node 1 to network card in node 1.
- Network card in node 1 to network card in node 2.
- Network in node 2 to CPU in node 2.
- CPU in node 2 to GPU in node 2.

Some companies such as Mellanox and NVIDIA recently have solved the problem by using GPUDirect RDMA, which can transfer data directly from GPU to GPU between the computers [18].

6.3. GPUDirect

GPUDirect allows multiple GPU devices to transfer data with no CPU intervention (eliminate internal copying and overhead by the host CPU). This can accelerate communication with network and make data transfer from GPU to communication network efficient. Allow peer-to-peer transfers between GPUs [19]. CUDA supports multiple GPUs communication, where data can be transferred between GPU devices without being buffered in CPU's memory, which can significantly speed up transfers and simplify programming [20]. **Figures 10** and **11** show how GPUDirect can be used in SHMD and MHMD, respectively.

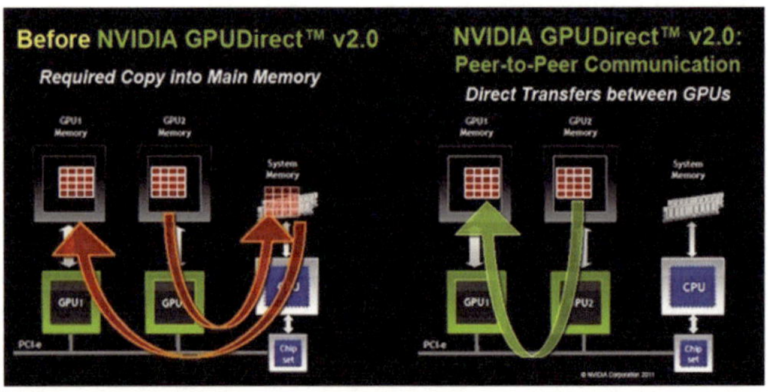

Figure 10. GPUDirect transfer in SHMD, from Ref. [19].

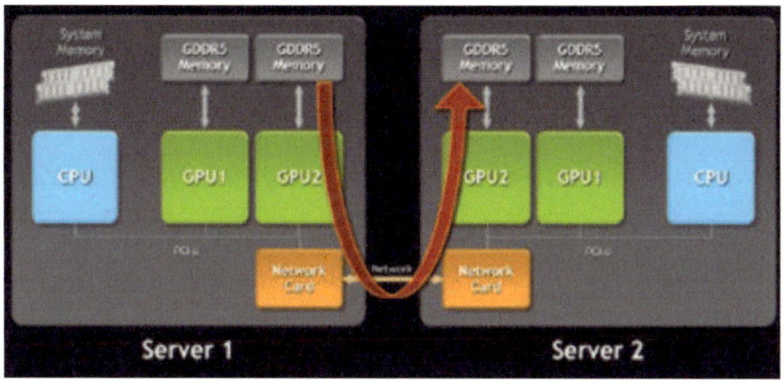

Figure 11. GPUDirect transfer in MHMD. Image from: http://www.paulcaheny.com/wp-content/uploads/2012/05/RDMA-GPU-Direct.jpg.

7. Tools for GPU computing

Many tools are available for developing GPU computing applications, including development environments, programming languages and libraries. In this section, we will give a little overview of some of these tools.

7.1. Compute unified device architecture (CUDA)

CUDA is a parallel computing platform and programming model invented by NVIDIA. It enables increases the computing performance by harnessing the power of the GPU devices. CUDA splits a problem into serial sections and parallel sections, serial sections are executed on the CPU as a host code and parallel sections are executed on the GPU by launching a kernel, **Figure 12**.

7.1.1. CUDA in SHSD

CUDA can run in SHSD using the following sequence of operations [21]:

- Declare and allocate host and device memory.
- Initialize host data.
- CPU transfer input data to GPU.
- Launch kernel on GPU to process the data in parallel.
- Copies results back from the GPU to the CPU.

Kernel code: the instructions actually executed on the GPU.

The following codes demonstrate a portion of code that can be run in SHSD.

```
//Kernel definition --- device code
__global__ void VecAdd(float* A, float* B, float* C)
{
int i = threadIdx.x;
C[i] = A[i] + B[i];
}
//////host code invoking kernel
int main() {
...
//Kernel invocation with N threads (invoke device code from host code)
VecAdd<<<1, N>>>(A, B, C);
...
}
```

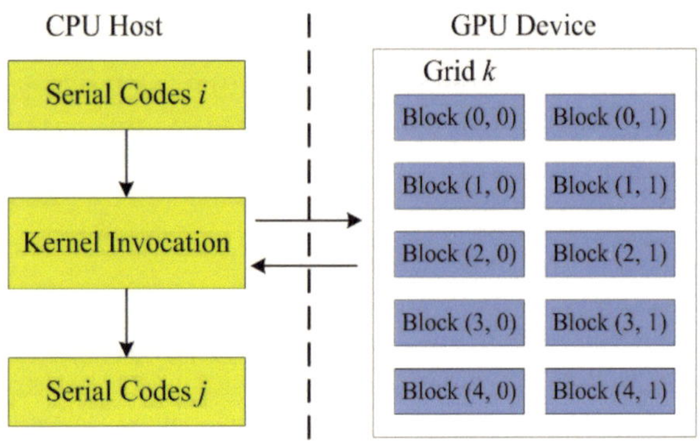

Figure 12. Using CUDA in SHSD. Image from: http://3dgep.com/wp-content/uploads/2011/11/Cuda-Execution-Model.png.

SHSD example from

7.1.2. CUDA in SHMD

The need for multiple GPUs is to gain more speed and overcome the limit of GPU device's memory (has smaller capacity compared to CPU's memory). For example, 32–64 GB is a typical size for the host memory, whereas a single GPU device has between 4 and 12 GB device memory. When dealing with large-scale scientific applications, the size of the device memory may thus become a limiting factor. One way of overcoming this barrier is to make use of multiple GPUs [22]. Now, systems with multiple GPUs are becoming more common. For SHMD, CUDA can manage multiple GPU devices from a single CPU host thread [23].

To use multiple GPU devices in single host, we need a thread for each device to control it (attach a GPU device to a host thread). The following codes show how one can invoke different kernels in different devices from a single host.

```
//Run independent kernel on each CUDA device
int numDevs = 0;
cudaGetNumDevices(&numDevs);//number of devices available
...
for (int d = 0; d < numDevs; d++) {
cudaSetDevice(d);//Attach a GPU device to a host thread (select a GPU)
kernel<<<blocks, threads>>>(args);//invoke independent kernel in each device
}
```

SHMD example using CUDA from Ref. [24]

7.1.3. Multiple host, single device (MHSD) and multiple host, multiple device (MHMD)

MPI is a programming model that used for a distributed memory system. If we have a MHSD or a MHMD system, MPI can be used to distribute tasks to computers, each of which can use their CPU and GPU devices to process the distributed task.

For example, if we want to do matrix multiplication on MHSD, then we can:

- Split the matrix into sub-matrices.
- Use MPI to distribute the sub-matrices to hosts (processes).
- Each host (process) can call a CUDA kernel to handle the multiplication on its GPU device(s).
- The result of multiplication would be copied back to each computer memory.
- Use MPI to gather results from all hosts (processes), and re-form the final matrix [25].

One way for programming MHSD and MHMD is to use MPI with CUDA, where MPI can be used to handles parallelization over hosts (nodes), and CUDA can be used to handle parallelization on devices (GPUs). We can use one MPI process per GPU and accelerate the computational kernels with CUDA.

For transferring data between different devices in different hosts, we can use the following steps:

- Sender: Copy data from a device to a temporary host buffer.
- Sender: Send host buffer data.
- Receiver: Receive data to host buffer.
- Receiver: Copy data to a device [26].

For example, if we need to transfer data between node 0 and node N-1 as shown in **Figure 13**, then we can use MPI_Send and MPI_Recv function as follows:

```
//MPI rank 0
MPI_Send(s_buf_d,size,MPI_CHAR,n-1,tag,MPI_COMM_WORLD);
//MPI rank n-1
MPI_Recv(r_buf_d,size,MPI_CHAR,0,tag,MPI_COMM_WORLD,&stat);
```

MHSD using MPI and CUDA

Where s_buf_d is from device 0 and r_buf_d is from device N-1.

The following code is a simple MPI with CUDA example that shows how to collect and print the list of devices from all MPI processes in the MHSD/MHMD system.

```
#include <stdlib.h>
#include <stdio.h>
#include <string.h>
#include <mpi.h>
#include <cuda.h>
#define MAX_NODES 100
#define BUFF_LEN 256
//Enumeration of CUDA devices accessible for the process.
void enumCudaDevices(char *buff)
{
char tmpBuff[BUFF_LEN];
int i, devCount;
cudaGetDeviceCount(&devCount);//number of devices
sprintf(tmpBuff," %3d", devCount);
strncat(buff, tmpBuff, BUFF_LEN);
for (i = 0; i < devCount; i++)
{
cudaDeviceProp devProp;
cudaGetDeviceProperties(&devProp, i);
sprintf(tmpBuff, " %d:%s", i, devProp.name);
strncat(buff, tmpBuff, BUFF_LEN);
}
}
int main(int argc, char *argv[])
{
int i, myrank, numprocs;
char pName[MPI_MAX_PROCESSOR_NAME],
buff[BUFF_LEN];
MPI_Init(&argc,&argv);
MPI_Comm_size(MPI_COMM_WORLD,&numprocs);
MPI_Comm_rank(MPI_COMM_WORLD, &myrank);
MPI_Get_processor_name(pName, &i);
sprintf(buff, "%-15s %3d", pName, myrank);
//Find local CUDA devices
enumCudaDevices(buff);
//Collect and print the list of CUDA devices from all MPI processes
if (myrank == 0)
{
char devList[MAX_NODES][BUFF_LEN];
```

```
MPI_Gather(buff, BUFF_LEN, MPI_CHAR,
devList, BUFF_LEN, MPI_CHAR,
0, MPI_COMM_WORLD);
for (i = 0; i < numprocs; i++)
printf("%s\n", devList + i);
}
else
MPI_Gather(buff, BUFF_LEN, MPI_CHAR,
NULL, 0, MPI_CHAR,
0, MPI_COMM_WORLD);
MPI_Finalize();
return 0;
}
```

The output of the program look similar to this:
g01n07.pdc.kth.se 0 3 0:Tesla M2090 1:Tesla M2090 2:Tesla M2090
g01n06.pdc.kth.se 1 3 0:Tesla M2090 1:Tesla M2090 2:Tesla M2090
MHMD simple example from
(https://www.pdc.kth.se/resources/software/old-installed-soft-ware/mpi-libraries/cuda-and-mpi)

Most recent versions of most MPI libraries support sending/receiving directly from CUDA device memory; for example Cray's implementation of MPICH supports passing GPU memory buffers directly to MPI function calls, without manually copying GPU data to the host before passing data through MPI. The following codes show how initialize memory on the GPU and then perform an MPI_Allgather operation between GPUs using device buffer [28].

```
#include <stdio.h>
#include <stdlib.h>
#include <cuda_runtime.h>
#include <mpi.h>
void main(int argc, char** argv)
{
MPI_Init (&argc, &argv);
int direct;
int rank, size;
int *h_buff = NULL;
int *d_rank = NULL;
int *d_buff = NULL;
size_t bytes;
int i;
//Ensure that RDMA ENABLED CUDA is set correctly
direct = getenv("MPICH_RDMA_ENABLED_CUDA")==NULL?0:atoi(getenv ("MPICH_RD
MA_ENABLED_CUDA"));
if(direct != 1){
printf ("MPICH_RDMA_ENABLED_CUDA not enabled!\n");
exit (EXIT_FAILURE);
```

```
}
//Get MPI rank and size
MPI_Comm_rank (MPI_COMM_WORLD, &rank);
MPI_Comm_size (MPI_COMM_WORLD, &size);
//Allocate host and device buffers and copy rank value to GPU
bytes = size*sizeof(int);
h_buff = (int*)malloc(bytes);
cudaMalloc(&d_buff, bytes);
cudaMalloc(&d_rank, sizeof(int));
cudaMemcpy(d_rank, &rank, sizeof(int), cudaMemcpyHostToDevice);
//Preform Allgather using device buffer
MPI_Allgather(d_rank, 1, MPI_INT, d_buff, 1, MPI_INT, MPI_COMM_WORLD);
//Check that the GPU buffer is correct
cudaMemcpy(h_buff, d_buff, bytes, cudaMemcpyDeviceToHost);
for(i=0; i<size; i++){
if(h_buff[i] != i) {
printf ("Alltoall Failed!\n");
exit (EXIT_FAILURE);
}
}
if(rank==0)
printf("Success!\n");
//Clean up
free(h_buff);
cudaFree(d_buff);
cudaFree(d_rank);
MPI_Finalize();
}
```

Direct transfer data, code from Ref. [28]

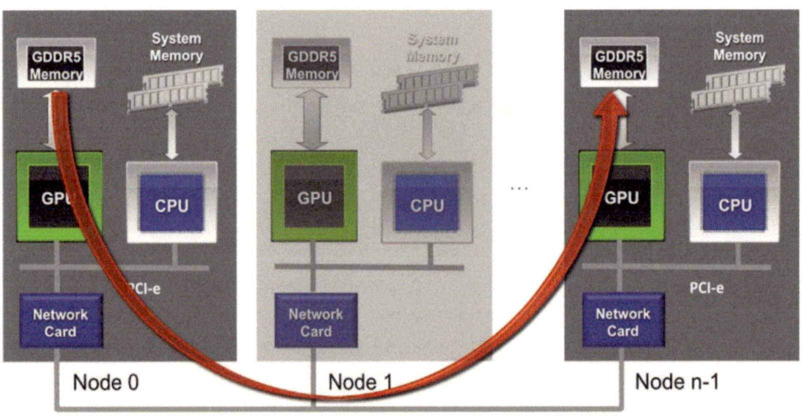

Figure 13. MPI with CUDA for MHSD, from Ref. [27].

http://dx.doi.org/10.5772/intechopen.68179

7.2. GPU computing using MATLAB

MATLAB is a widely used simulation tool for rapid prototyping and algorithm development. Since MATLAB uses a vector/matrix representation of data, which is suitable for parallel processing, it can benefit a lot from CPU and GPU cores.

We can use two tools for parallelization in MATLAB:

- Parallel computing toolbox: to run applications on SHSD and SHMD.
- Distributed computing server with parallel computing toolbox: for applications that will run in MHSD and MHMD.

7.2.1. Parallel computing toolbox

Parallel computing toolbox can be used to speed up MATLAB code by executing it on a GPU. There are more than 100 built-in functions in MATLAB that can be executed directly on the GPU by providing an input argument of the type GPUArray, a special array type provided by parallel computing toolbox. MATLAB GPU-enabled functions such as fft, filter and several linear algebra operations that can be used in GPU computing. In addition, there are other GPU-enabled functions in many toolboxes like image processing toolbox, communication system toolbox, statistics and machine learning toolbox, neural network toolbox, phased array systems toolbox and signal processing toolbox. So the CUDA kernel can be integrated in MATLAB applications by only a single line of MATLAB code [29].

Using MATLAB for GPU computing is good for those who have some or a lot of experience on MATLAB coding, but not enough depth in either C coding or the computer architecture for parallelization [30].

For example, FFT can be used to find the discrete Fourier transform of a vector of pseudorandom numbers on the CPU with normal arguments like this:

```
A = rand(2^16,1);
B = fft(A);
```

The same operation can be executed on the GPU by just using data type of gpuArray like this:

```
A = gpuArray(rand(2^16,1));

B = fft(A);
```

The result, B, is stored on the GPU. However, it is still visible in the MATLAB workspace. You can return the data back to the local MATLAB workspace by using gather command, for example, C = gather(B) [29].

7.2.2. MATLAB-distributed computing server

MATLAB-distributed computing server is suitable for MHSD and MHMD. The server provides access to multiple workers that receive and execute MATLAB code and Simulink models. Multiple users can run their applications on the server simultaneously.

MHSD and MHMD can use MATLAB workers in parallel computing toolbox and MATLAB-distributed computing server.

> MATLAB support CUDA-enabled NVIDIA GPUs with compute capability 2.0 or higher. For releases 14a and earlier, compute capability 1.3 is sufficient. In a future release, support for GPU devices of compute capability 2.x will be removed. At that time, a minimum compute capability of 3.0 will be required.

7.2.3. SHSD code examples

The following codes show how to perform matrix multiplication in SHSD.

```
Z = X*Y; % computation on CPU
x = gpuArray(X); % create copy from X on GPU
y = gpuArray(Y); % create copy from Y on GPU
z = x*y; % computation on GPU
ZZ = gather(z); % return data from GPU to CPU
```

Example 1: SHSD matlab code

The following codes using gpuArray to push data to GPU and then any function call on this array will be executed on GPU. To return result back from GPU device memory to host memory, we use gather function.

```
A = someArray(1000, 1000);
G = gpuArray(A); % Push to GPU memory
...
F = fft(G);
x = G\b;
...
z = gather(x); % Bring back into MATLAB
```

Example 2: SHSD code example, from Ref. [31]

7.2.4. SHMD code examples

In MTALAB, the parallel computing toolbox (PCT) can be used easily to perform computations on SHMD systems. PCT support CPU parallelism by using MATLAB pool. It allows you to use a number of workers run concurrently in the same time. The default number of workers is equal to the number of cores (for local pool). When you run a PARFOR loop, for example, then the work for that loop is broken up and executed by the MATLAB workers.

To perform computations in the SHMD system, you need to open a MATLAB pool with one worker for each GPU device. One MATLAB worker is needed to communicate with each GPU. Each MATLAB session can use one GPU at a time.

If you have only one GPU in your computer that GPU is the default. If you have more than one GPU device in your computer, you can use the gpuDevice function to select which device you want to use.

If you have 2 GPUs, you can assign one local worker for each device, as shown below:

```
matlabpool local 2 % two workers

spmd

gpuDevice(labindex); % select device for each work

g = gpuArray(...);

... operate on g...

End
```

SHMD (2)

7.2.5. Multiple host, single device (MHSD)/multiple host, multiple device (MHMD)

MATLAB® Distributed Computing Server™ lets you run computationally intensive MATLAB programs and Simulink® models on computer clusters, clouds and grids. You develop your program or model on a multicore desktop computer using parallel computing toolbox and then scale up to many computers by running it on MATLAB-distributed computing server. The server supports batch jobs, parallel computations and distributed large data. The server includes a built-in cluster job scheduler and provides support for commonly used third-party schedulers [32].

A parallel pool is a set of workers in a compute cluster (remote) or desktop (local). The default pool size and cluster are specified by your parallel preferences. The workers in a parallel pool can be used interactively and can communicate with each other during the lifetime of the job [33].

In the following multiple GPU example, we can have more than one workers: if the workers are local in the same host, then we can name this type as SHMD; if the workers are remote on cluster, then this means we are dealing with multiple hosts (MHs) and if there are more than one GPU device in each host (local workers in each remote host, with one worker for each remote GPU device, this can be multiple devices (MDs) and hence the system is MHMD; otherwise, it is MHSD.

```
N = 1000;
A = GPUaRRAY(a);
for ix = 1:N
x = myGPUFunction(ix,A)
xtotal(ix,:) = gather(x);
end
```

SHSD

```
N = 1000;
spmd
gpuDevice(labindex)%worker for each device
A = GPUaRRAY(A);
end
parfor ix = 1:N
x = myGPUFunction(ix,A)
xtotal(ix,:) = gather(x);
end
```

Multiple GPUs, from Ref. [32]

7.3. Open accelerator (OpenACC)

OpenACC is an application-programming interface, stands for open accelerators, it came to simplify parallel programming by providing a set of compiler directives that allow developers to run parallel code with the modifying underlying code (like OpenMP), and it was developed by CAPS, Cray, NVidia and PGI. OpenACC uses compiler directives that allow small segments of code, called kernels, to be run on the device. OpenACC divides tasks among gangs (blocks), gangs have workers (warps) and workers have vectors (threads) [9, 34–36].

OpenACC is portable across operating systems and various types of host CPUs and devices (accelerators). In OpenACC, some computations are executed in the CPU, while the compute intensive regions are offloaded to GPU devices to be executed in parallel. The host is responsible for

- allocation of memory in the device,
- initiating data transfer,
- sending the code to the device,
- waiting for completion,
- transferring the results back to the host,
- deallocating memory and
- queuing sequences of operations executed by the device [37].

A small code example for using OpenACC is as follow:

```
main()
{
<serial>
#pragma acc kernels
//automatically runs on GPU device
{
<parallel code>
}
}
```

#pragma acc kernels: tells the compiler to generate parallel accelerator kernels that run in parallel inside the GPU device [38].

8. Conclusion

In this chapter, taxonomy that divides GPU computing into four different classes was proposed. Class one (SHSD) and two (SHMD) are suitable for home GPU computing and can used to solve problems of single program and multiple data (SPMD) like image processing, where each task processes a part of the image, doing the same work in different data. The time spent in transferring data between the host and the device is affecting the overall performance, so try to minimize data transfer between the host and the device as possible as you can. Most successful GPU applications are doing a lot of computation in a small amount of data. This means, GPU will not work effectively for the small amount of threads, but it is efficiently launching many threads to use GPU effectively. It gives good performance when running a large number of threads in parallel.

Class three (MHSD) and four (MHMD) are used for GPU clustering, where data is transferred between devices on the same host or between devices in different hosts through a network connection. One of the reasons that affect performance is the speed of the used network.

Different types of GPU devices with different architectures and compute capabilities give different performance result, so choose the suitable one for your work before you start.

Author details

Abdelrahman Ahmed Mohamed Osman

Address all correspondence to: aamosman@uqu.edu.sa

Faculty of Computer at Al-Gunfudah, Umm AL-Qura University, Al-Gunfudah, Saudi Arabia

References

[1] Tanenbaum AS, Van Steen M. Distributed Systems. Prentice-Hall; © 2007 Pearson Education. Inc. Pearson Prentice Hall Pearson Education, Inc. Upper Saddle River, NJ 07458.

[2] Osman AAM. A multi-level WEB based parallel processing system a hierarchical volunteer computing approach. World Academy of Science, Engineering and Technology, International Journal of Computer, Electrical, Automation, Control and Information Engineering. 2008;**2**(1):176-181.

[3] Matloff N. Programming on Parallel Machines. Davis: University of California; 2011.

[4] Yuen DA, et al. GPU Solutions to Multi-scale Problems in Science and Engineering. Springer; 2013. http://www.springer.com/us/book/9783642164040

[5] Zahran M. Graphics Processing Units (GPUs): Architecture and Programming (Multi-GPU Systems) – Lecture. [cited January 9, 2017] [Internet]. Available from: http://cs.nyu.edu/courses/spring12/CSCI-GA.3033-012/lecture9.pdf

[6] NVIDIA. What is Gpu-Accelerated Computing. [Internet] 2016 [cited October 8, 2016]. Available from: http://www.nvidia.com/object/what-is-gpu-computing.html

[7] Cruz FA. Tutorial on GPU Computing With an Introduction to CUDA. [Internet] 2009 [cited January 10, 2017]. Available from: http://lorenabarba.com/gpuatbu/Program_files/Cruz_gpuComputing09.pdf

[8] An Introduction to Modern GPU Architecture, Ashu Rege, Director of Developer Techno logy NVIDIA. [cited December 31, 2016]. http://download.nvidia.com/developer/cuda/seminar/TDCI_Arch.pdf

[9] Kirk DB. W-mWH. Programming Massively Parallel Processors: A Hands-on Approach. Elsevier Inc. 2013.

[10] Rosenberg O. NVIDIA GPU Architecture: From Fermi to Kepler. Internet 2013 [cited January 15, 2017]. Available from: https://moodle.technion.ac.il/pluginfile.php/375213/mod_resource/content/1/Lecture%2313-FromFermitoKepler.pdf

[11] Vu Dinh DM. Graphics Processing Unit (GPU) Memory Hierarchy. Internet 2015 [cited January 3, 2017]. Available from: http://meseec.ce.rit.edu/551-projects/spring2015/3-2.pdf

[12] Harris, M. Tesla GPU Computing, A Revolution in High Performance Computing. Internet 2009 [cited January 3, 2017]. Available from: http://www.lsr.nectec.or.th/images/f/f2/Overview.pdf

[13] Kardos J. Efficient Data Transfer, Advanced Aspects of CUDA. Internet 2015 [cited January 3, 2017]. Available from: http://www.youtube.com/watch?v=Yv4thF9tvPo

[14] Rosenberg O. Introduction to GPU Architecture Internet [cited January 17, 2017]. Available from: http://haifux.org/lectures/267/Introduction-to-GPUs.pdf

[15] Evolution of PCI Express as the Ubiquitous I/O Interconnect Technology. Internet 2016 [cited January 17, 2017]. Published on Apr 8, 2016 In this video from the 2016 OpenFabrics Workshop, Debendra Das Shama presents: Available from: https://www.youtube.com/watch?v=eU5-6ogW1iY

[16] Fun and Easy PCIE – How the PCI Express Protocol works. 2016 [cited January 17, 2017]. Available from: https://www.youtube.com/watch?v=sRx2YLzBIqk

[17] Lawley J. Understanding Performance of PCI Express Systems. 2008. https://www.xilinx.com/support/documentation/white_papers/wp350.pdf

[18] How To Build and Use a Multi GPU System for Deep Learning 2014-09-21 by Tim Dettmers. Internet 2014 [cited January 17, 2017]. Available from: http://timdettmers.com/2014/09/21/how-to-build-and-use-a-multi-gpu-system-for-deep-learning/

[19] NVIDIA. GPUDirect. Internet [cited January 17, 2017]. Available from: https://developer.nvidia.com/gpudirect

[20] Marsden O. What is the Best Option for GPU Programming. Internet 2014 [cited January 14, 2017]. Available from: https://www.researchgate.net/post/What_is_the_best_option_for_GPU_programming

[21] Harris M. An Easy Introduction to CUDA C and C++. Internet 2012 [cited December 28, 2016]. Available from: https://devblogs.nvidia.com/parallelforall/easy-introduction-cuda-c-and-c/

[22] Sourouri M, et al. Effective multi-GPU communication using multiple CUDA streams and threads. In 2014 20th IEEE International Conference on Parallel and Distributed Systems (ICPADS). Hsinchu, Taiwan. IEEE: 2014.

[23] Micikevicius P. Multi-GPU Programming. Internet 2011 [cited December 29, 2016]. Available from: https://www.nvidia.com/docs/IO/116711/sc11-multi-gpu.pdf

[24] Harris MBM. CUDA Multi-GPU Programming Internet [cited February 19, 2017]. Available from: http://people.maths.ox.ac.uk/gilesm/cuda/MultiGPU_Programming.pdf

[25] Badgujar HY. How to Mix Mpi and Cuda in a Single program. Internet 2014 [cited February 19, 2017]. Available from: https://hemprasad.wordpress.com/2014/12/19 how-to-mix-mpi-and-cuda-in-a-single-program/

[26] Alfthan SV. Introduction GPU Computing. Internet 2011 [cited February 19, 2017]. Available from: http://www.training.prace-ri.eu/uploads/tx_pracetmo/GPU_intro.pdf

[27] Bernaschi M. Multi GPU Programming (With MPI) Internet 2014 [cited February 19, 2017]. Available from: http://twin.iac.rm.cnr.it/Multi_GPU_Programming_with_MPI.pdf; http://on-demand.gputechconf.com/gtc/2014/presentations/S4236-multi-gpu-programming-mpi.pdf

[28] Laboratory ORN. GPUDirect: CUDA aware MPI. Internet 2016 [cited February 19, 2017]. Available from: https://www.olcf.ornl.gov/tutorials/gpudirect-mpich-enabled-cuda/

[29] Jill Reese SZ. GPU Programming in MATLAB. Internet [cited February 14, 2017]. Available from: https://www.mathworks.com/company/newsletters/articles/gpu-programming-in-matlab.html

[30] Suh JW, Kim Y. Accelerating MATLAB with GPU Computing: A Primer with Examples. Newnes; Morgan Kaufmann; 2nd December 2013; 258. eBook ISBN: 9780124079168, Paperback ISBN: 9780124080805

[31] Dean L. GPU Computing with MATLAB. MATLAB Products MathWorks. 2010 [cited February 19, 2017]. http://on-demand.gputechconf.com/gtc/2010/presentations/S12267-GPU-Computing-with-Matlab.pdf

[32] Mathworks. MATLAB Distributed Computing Server. Internet 2016 [cited February 20, 2017]. Available from: https://www.mathworks.com/help/mdce/index.html

[33] Mathworks. What Is a Parallel Pool. Internet 2016 [cited February 20, 2017]. Available from: https://www.mathworks.com/help/distcomp/parallel-pools.html

[34] Zoran Dabic RL, Simonian E, Singh R, Tande S. An Introduction to OpenACCl. Internet [cited January 17, 2017]. Available from: http://heather.cs.ucdavis.edu/OpenACCDir/Intros158/DabicLutrellSimonianSinghTandel.pdf

[35] Rasmuss GMMNMR. An Introduction to OpenAcc ECS 158 Final Project Robert. Internet 2016 [cited January 17, 2017]. Available from: http://heather.cs.ucdavis.edu/OpenACCDir/Intros158/GonzalesMartinMittowRasmuss.pdf

[36] Killian W. An Introduction to OpenACC. 2013 Internet [cited January 17, 2017]. Available from: https://www.eecis.udel.edu/~wkillian/latest/resources/OpenACC.Lecture.CIS-C879.Spring2013.pdf

[37] Oscar Hernandez RG. Introduction to OpenACC. Internet 2012 [cited January 17, 2017]. Available from: https://www.olcf.ornl.gov/wp-content/training/electronic-structure-2012/IntroOpenACC.pdf

[38] Larkin J. An OpenACC Example. Internet 2012 [cited February 20, 2017]. Available from: https://devblogs.nvidia.com/parallelforall/openacc-example-part-1/

Chapter 5

Distributed Software Development Tools for Distributed Scientific Applications

Vaidas Giedrimas, Leonidas Sakalauskas and Anatoly Petrenko

Additional information is available at the end of the chapter

http://dx.doi.org/10.5772/intechopen.68334

Abstract

This chapter provides a new methodology and two tools for user-driven Wikinomics-oriented scientific applications' development. Service-oriented architecture for such applications is used, where the entire research supporting computing or simulating process is broken down into a set of loosely coupled stages in the form of interoperating replaceable Web services that can be distributed over different clouds. Any piece of the code and any application component deployed on a system can be reused and transformed into a service. The combination of service-oriented and cloud computing will indeed begin to challenge the way of research supporting computing development, the facilities of which are considered in this chapter.

Keywords: service computing, engineering tools, Wikinomics, mathematical programming, software modeling

1. Introduction

One of the factors on which the financial results of the business company depend is the quality of software which company is using. Scientific software plays even more special role. On its quality depend the reliability of the scientific conclusions and the speed of scientific progress. However, the ratio of successful scientific software projects is close to average: some part of the projects fails, some exceeds the budget, and some makes inadequate product.

The misunderstandings between scientists as end users and software engineers are even more frequent as usual. Software engineers have a lack of deep knowledge of user's domain (e.g., high energy physics, chemistry, and life sciences). In order to avoid possible problems, scientists sometimes try to develop "home-made" software. However, the probability of failure in such projects is even higher, because of the lack of the knowledge of software engineering domain. For example, scientists in common cases do not know good software engineering practices, processes, and so on. They even can have a lack of knowledge about good practices or good artefacts of the software, made by its colleagues.

We stand among the believers that this problem can be solved using the Wikinomics. The idea of Wikinomics (or Wiki economics) is introduced by Tapscott and Williams [15]. Wikinomics is the spatial activity, which helps to achieve the result, having available resources only. Wiki technologies are laid on very simple procedures: the project leaders collect critical mass of volunteers, who have a willing and possibilities to contribute in small scale. The sum of such small contributions gives huge contribution to the project result. The Wikipedia or Wikitravel portals can be presented as a success story of mass collaboration [17].

In other hand, we believe that the mass collaboration can help to improve only part of the scientific development process. We need a software developing solutions, oriented to services and clouds in order to use all available computational power of the distributed infrastructures.

Service-oriented computing (SOC) is extremely powerful in terms of the help for developer. The key point of modern scientific applications is a very quick transition from hypothesis generation stage to evaluating mathematical experiment, which is important for evidence and optimization of the result and its possible practical use. SOC technologies provide an important platform to make the resource-intensive scientific and engineering applications more significant [1–4]. So any community, regardless of its working area, should be supplied with the technological approach to build their own distributed compute-intensive multidisciplinary applications rapidly.

Service-oriented software developers work either as application builders (or services clients), service brokers, or service providers. Usually, the service repository is created which contains platform environment supporting services and application supporting services. The environment supporting services offer the standard operations for service management and hosting (e.g., cloud hosting, event processing and management, mediation and data services, service composition and workflow, security, connectivity, messaging, storage, and so on). They are correlated with generic services, provided by other producers (e.g., EGI (http://www.egi.eu/), Flatworld (http://www.flatworldsolutions. com/), FI-WARE (http://catalogue.fi-ware.org/enablers), SAP (http://www.sap.com/pc/tech/enterprise-information-management/), ESRC (http://ukdataservice. ac.uk/), and so on). Two dimensions of service interoperability, namely horizontal (communication protocol and data flow between services) and vertical matching (correspondence between an abstract user task and concrete service capabilities), should be supported in the composition process.

Modern scientific and engineering applications are built as a complex network of services offered by different providers, based on heterogeneous resources of different organizational structures. The services can be composed using orchestration or using choreography. If the orchestration is used, all corresponding Web services are controlled by one central web service. On the other hand, if the choreography is used and central orchestrator is absent, the services are independent in some extent. The choreography is based on collaboration and is mainly used to exchange messages in public business processes. As SOC developed, a number of languages for service orchestration and choreography have been introduced: BPEL4WS, BPML, WSFL, XLANG, BPSS, WSCI, and WSCL [5].

Our proposal has the following innovative features:

- Implementation of novel service-oriented design paradigm in distributed scientific application development area according to which all levels of research or design are divided into separate loosely coupled stages and procedures for their subsequent transfer to the form of standardized Web services.
- Creation of the repository of research application Web services which support collective research computing, simulating, and globalization of R&D activities.
- Adaption of the Wiki technologies for creation of the repository of scientific applications' source code, reusing existing software assets at the code level as well as at the Web services level.
- Personalization and customization of distributed scientific applications because users can build and adjust their research or design scenario and workflow by selecting the necessary Web services (as computing procedures) to be executed on cloud resources.

The rest of the paper is organized as follows: Section 2 presents overall idea of the platform for research collaborative computing (PRCC). Section 3 presents Web-enabled engineering design platform as one of the possible implementations of PRCC. Section 4 outlines the architecture, and main components of our other systems based on Wiki technologies. Section 5 describes the comparison of similar systems. Finally, the conclusions are made and future work discussed.

2. The platform for research collaborative computing

The service-oriented computing is based on the software services, which are platform-independent, autonomous, and computational elements. The services can be specified, published, discovered, and composed with other services using standard protocols. Such composition of services can be threat as wide-distributed software system. Many languages for software service composition are developed [5]. The goal of such languages is to provide formal way for specifying the connections and the coordination logic between services.

In order to support design, development, and execution of distributed applications in Internet environment, we have developed the end-user development framework called the platform for research collaborative computing. PRCC is an emerging interdisciplinary field, and it embraces physical sciences like chemistry, physics, biology, environmental sciences, hydrometeorology, engineering, and even art and humanities. All these fields are demanding for potent tools for mathematical modeling and collaborative computing research support. These tools should implement the idea of virtual organization including the possibility to combine distributed workflows, sequences of data processing functions, and so on. The platform for research collaborative computing is the answer for this demand. PRCC has the potential to benefit research in all disciplines at all stages of research. A well-constructed SOC can empower a research environment with a flexible infrastructure and processing environment by provisioning independent, reusable automated simulating processes (as services), and providing a robust foundation for leveraging these services.

PRCC concept is 24/7-available online intelligent multidisciplinary gateway for researchers supporting the following main users' activities: login, new project creation, creation of workflow, provision of input data such as computational task description and constrains, specification of additional parameters, workflow execution, and collection of data for further analysis.

User authorization is performed at two levels: for the virtual workplace access (login and password) and for grid/cloud resources access (grid certificate).

Application creating: Each customer has a possibility to create some projects, with services stored in the repository. Each application consists of a set of the files containing information about the computing workflow, the solved tasks, execution results, and so on.

Solved task description is allowed whether with the problem-oriented languages of the respective services or with the graphic editor.

Constructing of a computational route consists of choosing the computing services needed and connecting them in the execution order required. The workflow editor checks the compatibility of numerical procedures to be connected.

Parameters for different computational tasks are provided by means of the respective Web-interface elements or set up by default (except the control parameters, for instance, desirable value for time response, border frequencies for frequency analysis, and so on). It can be also required to provide type and parameters of output information (arguments of output characteristics, scale type used for plot construction and others).

Launch for executioninitiates a procedure of the application description generation in the internal format and its transferring to the task execution system. Web and grid service orchestrator are responsible for automatic route execution composed of the remote service invocation. Grid/cloud services invoked by the orchestrator during execution are responsible for preparing input data for a grid/cloud task, its launch, inquiring the execution state, unloading grid/cloud task results, and their transferring to the orchestrator.

Execution results consist of a set of files containing information on the results of computing fulfilled (according to the parameters set by a user) including plots and histograms, logs of the errors resulting in a stop of separate route's branches, ancillary data regarding grid/cloud resources used, and grid/cloud task executing. Based on the analysis of the received results, a customer could make a decision to repeat computational workflow execution with changed workflow's fragments, input data, and parameters of the computing procedures.

It is a need to know more details on services, its providers, and the customers, in order to manage service-oriented applications. There are two roles in development process: the role of service provider and the role of application builder. This separation of concerns empowers application architects to concentrate more on the business logic (in this case research). The technical details are left to service providers. Comprehensive repository of various services would ensure the possibility to use the services for the personal/institutional requirements of the scientific users via incorporation of existing services into widely distributed system (**Figure 1**).

Services can be clustered to two main groups: application supporting services (including subgroups: data processing services, modeling, and simulating services) and environment supporting (generic) services (including subgroups: cloud hosting for computational, network, and software resources provision, applications/services ecosystems and delivery framework, security, work-flow engine for calculating purposes, digital science services).

As far as authors know, there are no similar user-oriented platforms supporting experiments in mathematics and applied sciences. PRCC unveils new methodology for mathematical experiments planning and modeling. It can improve future competitiveness of the science by strengthening its scientific and technological base in the area of experimenting and data processing, which makes public service infrastructures and simulation processes smarter, i.e., more intelligent, more efficient, more adaptive, and sustainable.

2.1. Possible content of services' repository

Providing the ability to store ever-increasing amounts of data, making them available for sharing, and providing scientists and engineers with efficient means of data processing are the problems today. In the PRCC, this problem is solving by using the service repository

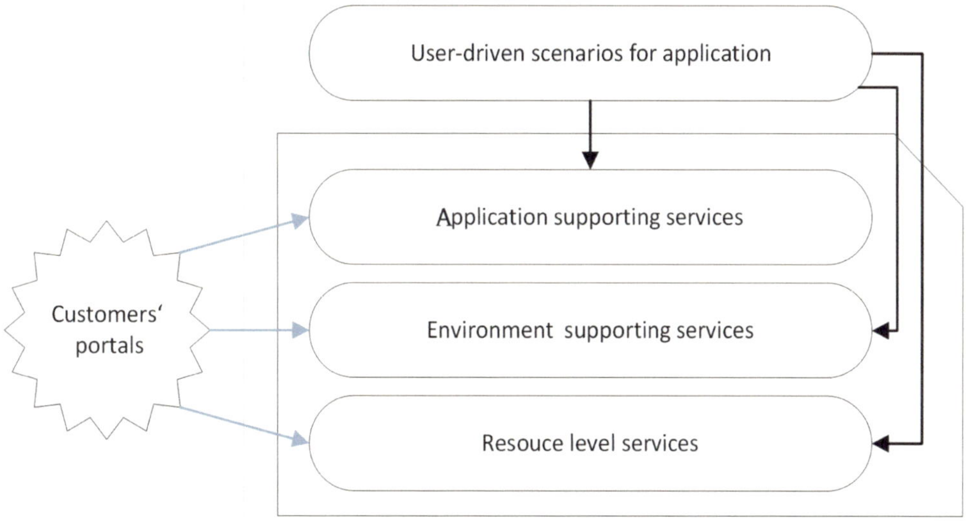

Figure 1. General structure of PRCC.

which is described here. From the beginning, it includes application supporting services (AS) for the typical scheme of a computational modeling experiment, been already considered.

Web services can contain program codes for implementation of concrete tasks from mathematical modeling and data processing and also represent results of calculations in grid/cloud e-infrastructures. They provide mathematical model equations solving procedures in depending on their type (differential, algebraic-nonlinear, and linear) and selected science and engineering analysis. Software services are main building blocks for the following functionality: data preprocessing and results postprocessing, mathematical modeling, DC, AC, TR, STA, FOUR and sensitivities analysis, optimization, statistical analysis and yield maximization, tolerance assignment, data mining, and so on. More detailed description of typical scheme of a computational modeling experiment in many fields of science and technology which has an invariant character is given in [3, 10]. The offered list of calculation types covers considerable part of possible needs in computational solving scientifically applied research tasks in many fields of science and technology.

Services are registered in the network service UDDI (Universal Description, Discovery, and Integration) which facilitate the access to them from different clients. Needed functionality is exposed via the Web service interface. Each Web service is capable to launch computations, to start and cancel jobs, to monitor their status, to retrieve the results, and so on.

Besides modeling tasks, there are other types of computational experiments in which distributed Web service technologies for science data analysis solutions can be used. They include in user scenario procedures of curve fitting and approximation for estimating the relationships among variables, classification techniques for categorizing different data into various folders, clustering techniques for grouping a set of objects in such a way that objects in the same group (cluster) are more similar to each other than to those in other groups, pattern recognition utilities, image processing, and filtering and optimization techniques.

Above computational Web services for data proceeding are used in different science and technology branches during data collection, data management, data analytics, and data visualization, where there are very large data sets: earth observation data from satellites; data in meteorology, oceanography, and hydrology; experimental data in physics of high energy; observing data in astrophysics; seismograms, earthquake monitoring data, and so on.

Services may be offered by different enterprises and communicate over the PRCC, that is why they provide a distributed computing infrastructure for both intra- and cross-enterprise application integration and collaboration. For semantic service discovery in the repository, a set of ontologies was developed which include *resource ontology* (hardware and software grid and cloud resources used for workflow execution), *data ontology* (for annotation of large data files and databases), and *workflow ontology* (for annotating past workflows and enabling their reuse in the future). The ontologies will be separated into two levels: generic ontologies and domain-specific ontologies. Services will be annotated in terms of their functional aspects such as IOPE, internal states (an activity could be executed in a loop, and it will keep track of its internal state), data transformation (e.g., unit or format conversion between input and output), and internal processes (which can describe in detail how to interact with a service, e.g., a service which takes partial sets of data on each call and performs some operation on the full set after last call).

2.2. Management of Web services

Service-oriented paradigm implies automated composition and orchestration of software services using workflows. Each workflow defines how tasks should be orchestrated and what components in what execution sequence should be. The workflow also includes the details of the synchronization and data flows. The workflow management may be based on standard Web-service orchestration description language WS-BPEL 2.0 (Business Process Execution Language). The initial XML-based description of the abstract workflow containing the task description parameters (prepared by user via the editor) is transformed to the WS-BPEL 2.0 description. Then, the orchestration engine invokes Web services passing this task description to them for execution.

The workflow management engine provides seamless and transparent execution of concrete workflows generated at the composition service. This engine leverages existing solutions to allow execution of user-defined workflows on the right combination of resources and services available through clusters, grids, clouds, or Web services. Furthermore, the project plans to work on the development of new scheduling strategies for workflow execution can be implemented that will take into account multicriteria expressions defined by the user as a set of preferences and requirements. In this way, workflow execution could be directed, for instance, to minimize execution time, to reduce total fee cost, or any combination of both.

The configuration and coordination of services in applications, based on the services, and the composition of services are equally important in the modern service systems [6]. The services interact with each other via messages. Message can be accomplished by using a template "request-response," when at a given time, only one of the specific services caused by one user (the connection between "one-to-one" or synchronous model); using a template "publish/subscribe" when on one particular event many services can respond (communications "one-to-many" or asynchronous model); and using intelligent agents that determine the coordination of services, because each agent has at its disposal some of the knowledge of the business process and can share this knowledge with other agents. Such a system can combine the quality of SOS, such as interoperability and openness, with MAS properties such as flexibility and autonomy.

3. Prototyping optimal design platform for engineering

The analysis of a state-of-art scientific platforms shows that there is a need of distributed computing-oriented platform. This obliges to redesign similar environments in the terms of separate interacting software services. So the designers should specify a workflow of the interaction of services.

Based on PRCC facilities, the Institute of Applied System Analysis (IASA) of NTUU "Kiev Polytechnic Institute" (Ukraine) has developed the user case WebALLTED[1] as the Web-enabled engineering design platform, intended, in particular, for modeling and optimization of nonlinear dynamic systems, which consist of the components of different physical nature and which are widely spread in different scientific and engineering fields. It is the cross-disciplinary application for distributed computing.

Developed engineering service-oriented simulation platform consists of the following layers (**Figure 2**). The most important features of this architecture are the following: Web accessibility, the distribution of the functionality across the software services in e-infrastructure, the compatibility with existing protocols and standards, the support of user-made scenarios in

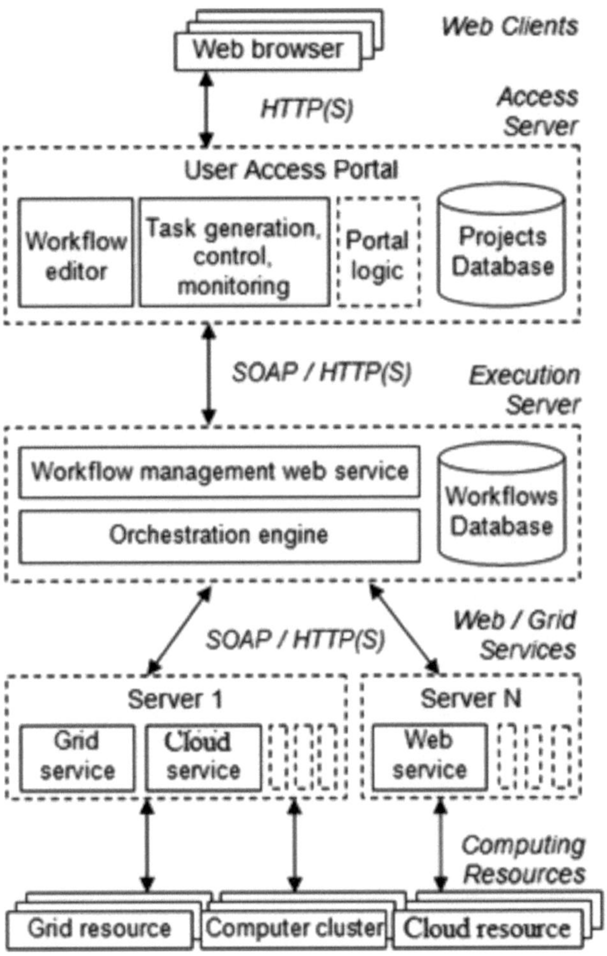

Figure 2. Main elements of SOA in the engineering simulation system.

[1]ALLTED means ALL TEchnologies Designer [7, 8].

development-time and in run-time, and the encapsulation of the software services interaction complexity.

The following functions are accessible via user interface: authentication, workflow editor, artefacts repository management environment, task monitoring, and more. The server side of the system is designed as multitier one in order to implement the workflow concept described early. First-access tier is the portal supporting user environment. The purpose of its modules is the following: the user-input-based generation of abstract workflow specification; the transition of task specification to lower tiers, where the task will be executed; and the postprocessing of results including saving the artefacts in DB.

The workflow manager works as second-execution tier. It is deployed in the execution server. The purpose of this tier is the mapping of the abstract workflow specification to particular software services. The orchestration is done using the specific language similar to WS-BPEL for BPEL instruments. The workflow manager starts executing particular workflow with the external orchestrator as well as observes the state of workflow execution and procures its results.

Particular workflow is working with functional software services and performs the following actions: data preprocessing and postprocessing, simulation, optimization, and so on. If high demand for resources is forecasted, only one node could be loaded to heavy. So the computation is planned on separate nodes and hosting grid/cloud services. These services give possibility to use widespread infrastructure (such as grid or cloud). It is possible to modify and to introduce of new functions to the system. This is done by the user by selection or registration of another Web or grid/cloud services.

The user is able to start the task in an execution tier. Task specification is transient to the service of workflow management. This abstract workflow is transformed to the particular implementation on execution server. Then, the workflow manager analyses the specification, corrects its possible errors (in some extent), demands the data about the services from the repository, and performs binding of activity sequence and software services calls. For the arrangement of software services in correct invocation order, the Mapper unit is used in the workflow. It initializes XML messages, variables, etc., and provides the means for the control during a run-time including the observing of workflow execution, its cancelling, early results monitoring, and so on. Finally, the orchestrator executes this particular "script."

User is informed about the progress of the workflow execution by monitoring unit communicating with workflow manager. When execution is finished, the user can retrieve the results, browse and analyze them, and repeat this sequence if needed.

The architecture hides the complexity of web-service interaction from user with abstract workflow concept and simple graphical workflow editor (**Figure 3**).

Web services are representing the basic building blocks of simulation system's functionality, and they enable customers to build and adjust scenarios and workflows of their design procedures or mathematical experiments via the Internet by selecting the necessary Web services, including automatic creation of equations of a mathematical model (an object or a process)

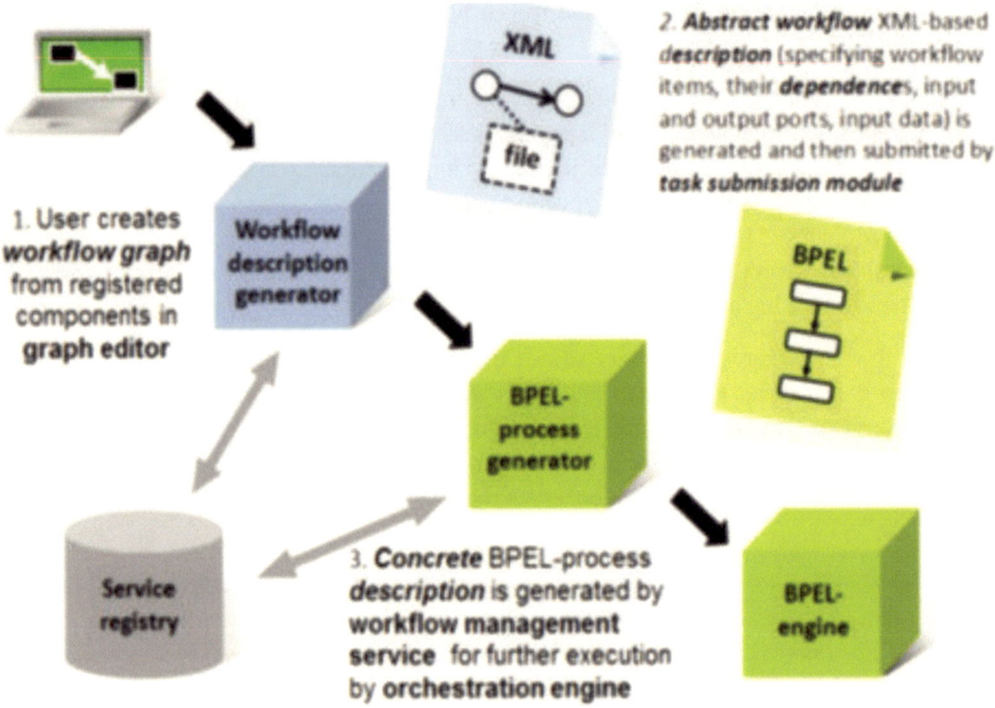

Figure 3. WebALLTED graphical workflow editor.

based on a description of its structure and properties of the used components, operations with large-scale mathematical models, steady-state analysis, transient and frequency-domain analysis, sensitivity and statistical analysis, parametric optimization and optimal tolerance assignment, solution centering, yield maximization, and so on [3].

Computational supporting services are based mostly on innovative numeric methods and can be composed by an end user for workflow execution on evaluable grid/cloud nodes [3]. They are oriented, first of all, on Design Automation domain, where simulation, analysis, and design can be done for different electronic circuits, control systems, and dynamic systems composed of electronic, hydraulic, pneumatic, mechanical, electrical, electromagnetic, and other physical phenomena elements.

The developed methodology and modeling toolkit support collective design of various micro-electro-mechanical systems (MEMS) and different microsystems in the form of chips.

4. Distributed Wiki-based system for stochastic programming and modeling

As is mentioned above, even empowered by huge computing power accessible to via Web services and clouds, users have still not exhausted possibilities, because of the lack of communication. Only communication and legal reuse of existing software assets in addition to available computing power can ensure high speed of scientific activities. In this section is described another distributed scientific software development system, which is developed in parallel and independently from the system described in Section 4. However, both of these are sharing similar ideas.

4.1. The architecture of stochastic programming and modeling system

We are started from the following hypothesis: the duration of development of scientific software can be decreased, the quality of such software can be improved using together with the power of the grid/cloud infrastructure, Wiki-based technologies, and software synthesis methods. The project was executed via three main stages:

- The development of the portal for the Wiki-based mass collaboration. This portal is used as the user interface in which scientists can specify software development problems, can rewrite/refine the specifications and software artefacts given by its (remote) colleagues, and can contribute all the process of software development for particular domain. The set of the statistical simulation and optimization problems was selected as the target domain for pilot project. In the future, the created environment can be applied to other domains as well.
- The development of the interoperability model in order to bridge Wiki-based portal and the Lithuanian National Grid Infrastructure (NGI-LT) or other (European) distributed infrastructures. A private cloud based on Ubuntu One is created at Siauliai University within the framework of this pilot project.
- To refine existing methods for software synthesis using the power of distributed computing infrastructures. This stage is under development yet, so it is not covered by this chapter. More details and early results are exposed in [22] (**Figure 4**).

The system for stochastic programming and statistical modeling based on Wiki technologies (WikiSPSM) consists of the following parts (**Figure 1**):

- Web portal with the content management system as the graphical user interface.
- Server-side backed for tasks scheduling and execution.
- Software artefacts (programs, subroutines, models, etc.) storage and management system.

The user interface portal consists of four main components:

- Template-based generator of Web pages. This component helps user to create web page content using template-based structure. The same component is used for the storage and version control of generated Web pages.
- WYSIWYG text editor. This editor provides more functionality than simple text editor on the Web page. It is dedicated to describe mathematical models and numerical algorithms. This component is enriched with the text preprocessing algorithms, which prevents from the hijacking attacks and code injection.

- The component of IDE (integrated developing environment) is implemented for the software modeling and code writing.
- The repository of mathematical functions. This component helps user to retrieve, rewrite, and append the repository of mathematical functions with new artefacts. WikiSPSM system is using NetLib repository LAPACK API; however, it can be improved on demand and can use other libraries, e.g., ESSL (Engineering Scientific Subroutine Library) or Parallel ESSL [16].

WikiSPSM is easy extensible and evolvable because of the architectural decision to store all the mathematical models, algorithms, programs, and libraries in central database.

Initially, it was planned that WikiSPSM will enable scientific users to write their software in C/C++, Java, Fortran 90, and QT programming languages. Because of this, the command-line interface is chosen as the architecture of communication between the UI and software generator part. Software generator performs the following functions: compilation, task submission (to distributed infrastructure or to single server), task monitoring, and control of the tasks and their results. For the compilation of the programs, we have chosen external command-

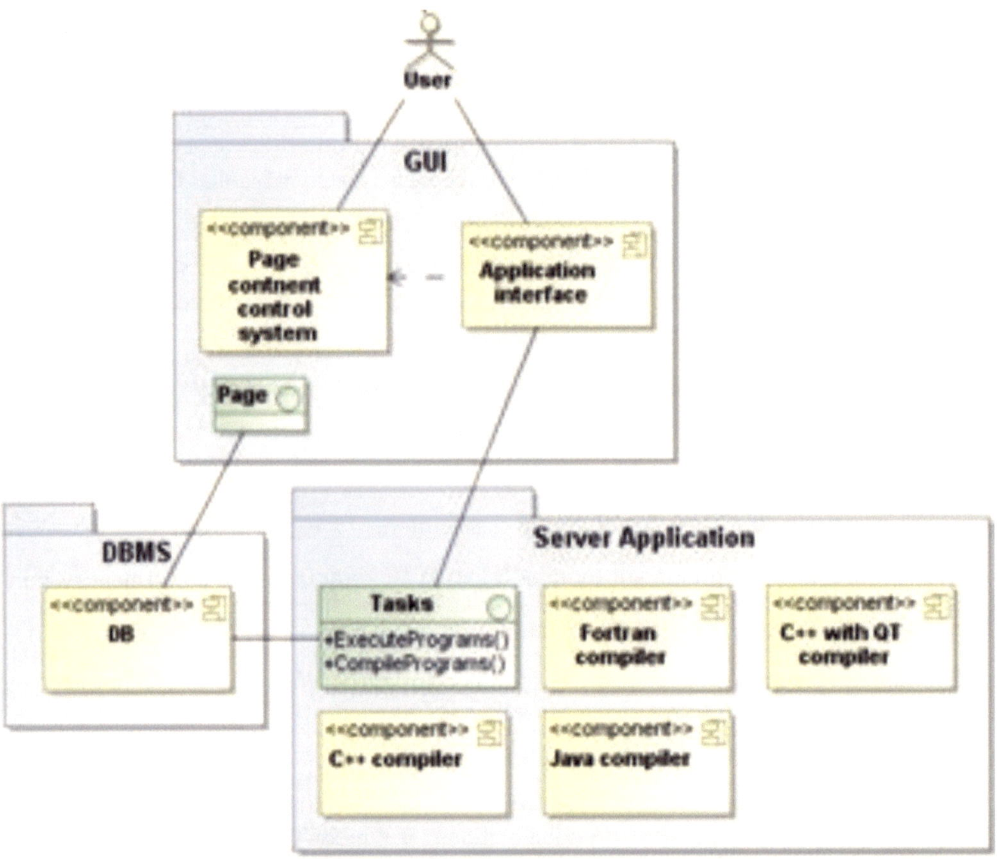

Figure 4. Main components of the Wiki-based stochastic programming and statistical modeling system.

line compilers. The architecture of the system lets to change its configuration and to work with another programming language having related SDK with command-line compiler. The users also are encouraged to use command-line interfaces instead of GUI. Latest version of WikiSPSM does not support application with GUI interfaces. This is done because of two factors: (a) many scientific applications are command-line-based and the graphical representation of the data is performed with other tools; (b) the support of GUI gives more constraints for scientific application.

In early versions of WikiSPSM, the compilation and execution actions were made in server side.[2] Object server creates an object task for each submitted data array received from the portal. Task object parses the data and sends back to user (via portal). For tasks monitoring, results getting the token are used. After the finishing of task, it transfers the data to server object. After that it is time for the compilation and execution. Each task is queued and scheduled. If it is not sufficient amount of resources (e.g., working nodes), task is laid out to the waiting queue. When the task is finished, its results are stored in DB (**Figure 4**).

4.2. Bridge to distributed systems

Soon after first test of WikiSPSM was observed, that client-server architecture does not fit the demands on computational resources. Increased number of users and tasks have negative impact on the performance of overall system. The architecture of the system has been changed in order to solve this issue.

In current architecture, the component for software generation was changed. This change was performed via two stages:

- Transformation between different OSs.[3] The server side of previous version was hardly coupled with OS (in particular, Windows). It was based on Qt API and command-line compilers. This fragment was reshaped completely. New implementation is Linux oriented, so now WikiSPSM can be considered as multiplatform tool.
- Transformation between the paradigms. In order to ensure better throughput of computing application, server was redesigned to schedule tasks in distributed infrastructures. Ubuntu One and Open Stack private clouds were chosen for the pilot project (**Figure 5**). Distributed file system NFS is used for the communication of working nodes.

Tests of redesigned component show very good results. For example, for 150 tasks, Monte-Carlo problem using new (bridged to distributed systems) execution component was solved in two times faster than initial server-based application component. The "toy example" (calculation of the factorial of big numbers) was solved eight times faster.

More comprehensive information about WikiSPSM could be found in Ref. [11, 12, 20, 21].

[2]Server side" here means general backend including cloud also.
[3]OS—the operating system.

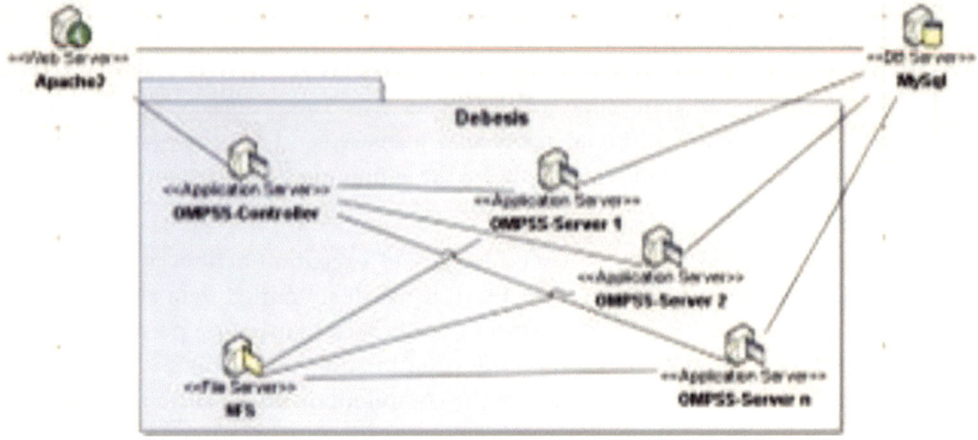

Figure 5. The architecture of WikiSPSM with the cloud computing component.

5. Related work

As far as authors of the chapter know the conception of Engineering, SOC with design procedures as Web services has almost no complete competitors worldwide [3]. However, partial comparison to other systems is possible.

The original numerical algorithms are in the background of WebALLTED [3, 7, 8, 9], e.g., algorithms for analysis of steady or transient state, frequency, algorithms for parametrical optimization, yield maximization, and so on. The proposed approach to application design is completely different from present attempts to use the whole indivisible applied software in the grid/cloud infrastructure as it is done in Cloud SME, TINACloud, PartSim, RT-LAB, FineSimPro, and CloudSME.

WebALLTED was compared to SPICE. The following positive features of WebALLTED were observed:

- Improvements on simulation rapidity and numerical convergence;
- Inclusive procedure of optimization and tolerance threshold setting;
- Sensitivity of analysis tools;
- Different approach of the determination of secondary response parameters (e.g., delays);
- Richer possibilities to perform user-defined modeling;
- Novel way of generate a system-level model of MEMS from FEM component equations (e.g., being received by means of ANSYS) [7];
- Dynamicity of the software architecture configuration in the terms of composed services and working nodes.

For evaluation the possibilities of WikiSPSM, it has been compared to other commercial (Mathematica) and open-source (Scilab) products. All compared products support rich set of mathematical functions; however, Mathematica's list of functions [13, 18] is most distinguishing for the problems of mathematical programming. WikiSPSM uses NetLib repository LAPACK [19] for C++ and FORTRAN, so they provide more functionality as Scilab [14]. In contrast to Mathematica and Scilab, WikiSPSM cannot reuse its functions directly, because it is Web based, and all the programs are executed on the server side, not locally. However, WikiSPSM shows best result by the possibility to extend system repository. Other systems have different single-user-oriented architecture. Moreover, they have only a little possibility to change system functions or extend the core of the system by user subroutines.

6. Conclusions

The following conclusion can be made:

- The analysis of a current state of scientific software development tools proves the urgent need of existing tools re-engineering to enable their operation in distributed computing environments.
- The original concept of the service-oriented distributed scientific applications development (with computing procedures as Web services) has the following innovative features:
    - Division of the entire computational process into separate loosely coupled stages and procedures for their subsequent transfer to the form of unified software services;
    - Creation of a repository of computational Web services which contains components developed by different producers that support collective research application development and globalization of R&D activities;
    - Separation services into environment supporting (generic) services and application supporting services;
    - Unique Web services to enable automatic formation of mathematical models for the solution tasks in the form of equation descriptions or equivalent substituting schemes;
    - Personalized and customized user-centric application design enabling users to build and adjust their design scenario and workflow by selecting the necessary Web services to be executed on grid/cloud resources;
    - Re-composition of multidisciplinary applications can at runtime because Web services can be further discovered after the application has been deployed;
    - Service metadata creation to allow meaningful definition of information in cloud environments for many service providers which may reside within the same infrastructure by agreement on linked ontology;
    - The possibility to collaborate using Wiki technologies and reuse software at code level as well as at service level.
- The prototype of the service-oriented engineering design platform was developed on the base of the proposed architecture for electronic design automation domain. Beside EDA the simulation, analysis and design can be done using WebALLTED for different control systems and dynamic systems.

- The prototype of collaboration-oriented stochastic programming and modeling system WikiSPMS was developed on the base of Wiki technologies and open-source software.

We believe that the results of the projects will have direct positive impact in the scientific software development, because of the bridging two technologies, each of them promises good performance. The power of the Wiki technologies, software services, and clouds will ensure the ability of the interactive collaboration on software developing using the terms of particular domain.

Author details

Vaidas Giedrimas[1]*, Leonidas Sakalauskas[1,2] and Anatoly Petrenko[3]

*Address all correspondence to: vaigie@mi.su.lt

1 Siauliai University, Siauliai, Lithuania

2 Vilnius University, Vilnius, Lithuania

3 National Technical University of Ukraine "Kyiv Polytechnic Institute", Kiyv, Ukraine

References

[1] Chen Y, Tsai W-T. Distributed Service-Oriented Software Development. Kendall Hunt Publishing; Iowa, USA. 2008. p. 467

[2] Papazoglou MP, Traverso P, Dustdar S, Leymann F. Service-oriented computing: A research roadmap. International Journal of Cooperative Information Systems. 2008;**17**(2):223-255

[3] Petrenko AI. Service-oriented computing (SOC) in a cloud computing environment. Computer Science and Applications. 2014;**1**(6):349-358

[4] Kress J, Maier B, Normann H, Schmeidel D, Schmutz G, Trops B, Utschig-Utschig C, Winterberg T. Industrial SOA [Internet]. 2013. Available from: http://www.oracle.com/technetwork/articles/soa/ind-soa-preface-1934606.html [Accesed: 2017-01-30]

[5] OASIS. OASIS Web Services Business Process Execution Language [Internet]. 2008. Available from: https://www.oasis-open.org/committees/tc_home.php?wg_abbrev=wsbpel [Accessed 2017-06-01]

[6] Petrenko AA. Comparing the types of service systems architectures [in Ukrainian]. System Research & Information Technologies. 2015;**4**:48-62

[7] Zgurovsky M, Petrenko A, Ladogubets V, Finogenov O, Bulakh B. WebALLTED: Interdisciplinary simulation in grid and cloud. Computer Science (Cracow). 2013; **14**(2):295-306

[8] Petrenko A, Ladogubets V, Tchkalov V, Pudlowski Z. ALLTED—A Computer-Aided System for Electronic Circuit Design. Melbourne: UICEE (UNESCO); 1997. p. 204

[9] Petrenko AI. Macromodels of micro-electro-mechanical systems. In: Islam N, editor. Microelectro-Mechanical Systems and Devices. InTech Rijeka, Croatia; 2012. pp. 155-190

[10] Petrenko AI. Collaborative complex computing environment (Com-Com). Journal of Computer Science and Systems Biology. 2015;**8**:278-284. DOI: 10.4172/jcsb.1000201

[11] Giedrimas V, Sakalauskas L, Žilinskas K. Towards the Environment for Mass-Collaboration for Software Synthesis, EGI User Forum [Internet]. 2011. Available from: https://indico.egi.eu/indico/event/207/session/15/contribution/117/material/slides/0.pdf [Accessed 2016-09-15]

[12] Giedrimas V, Varoneckas A, Juozapavicius A. The grid and cloud computing facilities in Lithuania. Scalable Computing: Practice and Experience. 2011;**12**(4):417-421

[13] Steinhaus S. Comparison of mathematical programs for data analysis. Munich; 2008. http://www.newsciencecore.com/attach/201504/09/173347uyziem4evkr0i405.pdf last accesed : 2017-06-11

[14] Baudin M. Introduction to Scilab. The Scilab Consortium; 2010

[15] Bunks C, Chancelier J-P, Delebecque F, Gomez C, Goursat M, Nikoukhah R, Steer S. Engineering and Scientific Computing with Scilab. Boston: Birkhauser; 1999

[16] ESSL and Parallel ESSL Library [Internet]. IBM, 2016. Available from: https://www-03.ibm.com/systems/power/software/essl/ [Accessed 2017-06-01]

[17] Tapscott D, Williams AD. Wikinomics: How Mass Collaboration Changes Everything. Atlantic Books, London; 2011

[18] Wolfram Research. Wolfram gridMathematica: Multiplying the power of Mathematica over the grid. [Internet]. 2006. Available from: http://www.wolfram.com/gridmathematica/ [Accessed 2017-06-11]

[19] Barker VA, et al. LAPACK User's Guide: Software, Environments and Tools. Society for Industrial and Applied Mathematics; Philadelphia, USA. 2001

[20] Sakalauskas L. Application of the Monte-Carlo method to nonlinear stochastic optimization with linear constraints. Informatica. 2004;**15**(2):271-282

[21] Giedrimas V, Sakalauskas L, Žilinskas K, Barauskas N, Neimantas M, Valčiukas R. Wiki-based stochastic programming and statistical modelling system for the cloud. International Journal of Advanced Computer Science & Applications. 2016;**7**(3): 218-223

[22] Giedrimas V. Distributed systems for software engineering: Non-traditional approach. In: Proceedings of the 7th International Conference on Application of Information and Communication Technologies (AICT 2013). Baku (Azerbaijan), 23-25 October. Published by Institute of Electrical and Electronics Engineers (IEEE); 2013. pp. 31-34

Chapter 6

DANP-Evaluation of AHP-DSS

Wolfgang Ossadnik, Ralf H. Kaspar and
Benjamin Föcke

Additional information is available at the end of the chapter

http://dx.doi.org/10.5772/67130

Abstract

The analytic hierarchy process (AHP) and the analytic network process (ANP) are important multi-criteria decision-making (MCDM) methods for solving strategic decision problems. In the field of the research and teaching projects of a university's Management Science Department, the use of adequate decision support systems (DSS) enables an appropriate application and acceptance of these methods. By reason of the great variety of AHP-DSS, the aim of this paper is the selection of AHP-supporting software. Owing to the interdependencies of the software quality criteria, these influences can be evaluated appropriately by the ANP. As for the various requirements of the different department members, the ANP procedure is linked with the DEMATEL approach. Within such a combined framework (DANP), the alternate software products and their quality selection criteria are transparently analysed and evaluated from a multi-personal point of view. The described procedure is an object of reference to solve such structuring and evaluation problems by support of parallel and/or distributed computing architecture.

Keywords: analytic hierarchy process (AHP), analytic network process (ANP), DEMATEL, DSS evaluation, parallel and distributed computing

1. Introduction

In the field of academic teaching and research, the multi-criteria decision-making (MCDM) methods gain ongoing increasing importance. In many lectures, seminaries, exercises, tutorials, papers, etc., these methods are presented, and decision support systems (DSS) are applied. The same applies to academic research and paper production. Within this context, the analytic hierarchy process (AHP) and the analytic network process (ANP) are regarded as important MCDM methods to solve strategic decision problems. Additionally, the impact of these two methods in the literature is continuously growing. Thereby, working with these methods and embedding them into the systematic environment of an adequate DSS becomes undeniable for students and academic staff.

Despite the comparatively less sophisticated mathematical computation of the more popular AHP, it is necessary to secure an efficient application of this method by a suitable DSS. By this, a correct implementation of this method is brought forward and the acceptance of academic staff and students can be boosted. On this background, the paper presents five substantially varying AHP-DSS, evaluated by five members of a Management Science Department of a medium-sized university. These persons have different profiles in academic teaching and research experiences, requirements and preferences. Based on standard criteria of ISO/IEC 25010 to evaluate the quality of software products, modified criteria were customized to the specificity of AHP software products and the demands of a Management Science Department. To cope with (inter-)dependencies of the evaluation criteria, the ANP is used as evaluation method and supported by DEMATEL to reconsider the wide range of requirements of the different department members. As a contribution to the field of ANP application, the DANP procedure is transparently shown. Furthermore, the implications of more network complexity and of an enhancing number of experts with diverging software quality requirements regarding a demand for parallel and/or distributed computing architectures are subsequently focused.

The remainder of the chapter is organized as follows: Section 2 provides a critical overview of AHP's and ANP's conceptual foundations in the field of discrete strategic decision problems. Furthermore, the necessity of using DSS is pointed out. Section 3 is devoted to the research framework and the evaluation of AHP-DSS with DANP followed by considerations on a possible support by parallel and distributed computing (Section 4). The chapter ends with a summary of the main results of the study as well as with concluding remarks and future prospects (Section 5).

2. Applying AHP and ANP in a Management Science Department

One of the fundamental tasks of Management Science is the support of complex managerial decision problems. For this purpose, information and supporting methodology relevant to the decision-making process must be made available. This applies particularly to the field of future-oriented strategic decision settings which require top management, involve the allocation of a large amount of resources, are likely to have a significant impact on the long-term prosperity of the company with major consequences and necessitate to consider internal and external environmental factors [1]. Academic teaching and research in business has to take these requirements into account and to embed these decision problems in a multidimensional decision system with diverging goals. This task can be induced by multiple top-goals (to be sufficed in a not-for-profit organization) or an analogous structure of the relationship between multiple causes and one intended financial effect in the context of the steering tasks of a traditional entrepreneurial organization and its cause-and-effect structure relevant for financial performance generation.

The analysis of multiple goal decision problems has evolved continuously over recent decades, primarily in the field of operations research (OR) beginning with goal programming [2–4].

In business, OR is an important support for decision-making by available adequate MCDM methods. Such methods are becoming increasingly important for decision support functions. The results of a performed MCDM related bibliometric study [5] revealed that AHP [6–9] and ANP [10–13] are two of the most adequate decision support methods and the most important MADM approaches for solving complex discrete decision problems. Comparative advantages of both methods are for instance that they are able to cope with quantitative and qualitative criteria by the possibility of considering ordinal and cardinal judgements, with the involvement of more than one decision maker and the ongoing development of efficient software support.

Within the AHP, decision problems have to be structured in a clear and unambiguous hierarchy with an overall goal, sub-goals, criteria and alternatives. The ANP—as a more general form of the AHP—exceeds the AHP by the possibility to consider dependence and feedback between criteria referring to the problem.

With respect to the complexity of strategic management decisions which can be disassembled into variety (number and type of elements) and connectivity (number and type of relations between the elements), there can be distinguished between managerial decision problems with a lower and a higher degree of complexity. As the variety of elements is not influencing the choice between AHP and ANP due to the fact that both approaches can handle a lot of different decision elements at the same time, the focus lies on the connectivity aspect of a decision environment. If there is a lower level of complexity with a manageable amount of dependencies in a hierarchic structure, the AHP can be used. In the case of higher complexity (increasing connectivity) with more horizontal dependencies, the ANP is the adequate decision support technique.

Even though many complex strategic decision settings can be depicted through a network structure, an ANP model must not yield better results than using the AHP [14]. Using hierarchies (as structural characteristic of the AHP) has furthermore the advantage that this system can be used to describe changes in priority on higher levels affect the priority of elements on lower levels. Constraints of the elements on a level are represented on the next higher level to ensure that they are met. Moreover, hierarchies are stable and flexible which means that small changes cause small effects and that additions to a well-structured hierarchy do not disrupt the performance [6, 7].

The AHP can support complex strategic decisions, e.g. the selection of new suppliers, locations of production plants or capital goods of any kind [5]. By contrast, the ANP should be used in case of interdependencies between criteria, for instance, to be reconsidered in means-end-relationships for organizational policy on the basis of the cause-and-effect structure of the financial performance generation. In comparison to ANP, the AHP is furthermore more popular because of less complexity during the modelling process and on the other hand due to less sophisticated mathematical requirements. But nevertheless, AHP-DSS are necessary for an adequate application of the method and its acceptance by scholars and managers. As DSS comprise a wide spectrum of characteristics, it is important to select a product adequate to requirements which will vary within a Management Science Department according to different persons and their functions. Therefore, our aim is a transparent evaluation of selected AHP-DSS in a multi-personally organized process.

As the relevance of the AHP for scientists and practitioners is proved in bibliometric studies [5, 15], a need for AHP-adequate software support for these groups of persons is comprehensible. The question is first of all, if such software products should be evaluated and selected by AHP or by ANP?

Even though AHP-based evaluations of AHP-software exist [16–18], it is to be considered that some criteria relevant for quality estimation of AHP-oriented software products in academic departments do not seem to be independent from each other. Therefore, it seems to be an appropriate option to use ANP for our evaluation.

As there is no ANP-based evaluation of AHP-software to be found in the literature, which might support our software evaluation problem, an own tailor-made process of selecting AHP software, adequate to the research and teaching requirements and demands of a Management Science Department was developed.

3. DANP-evaluation of AHP-DSS

3.1. Selection of AHP-DSS

Owing to the wide range of software solutions supporting AHP application [17], the selection of software has to be conducted first, whereby initially all products are relevant which are freeware or are ensuring a free trial access for evaluation purposes (at least for a limited time period). Regarding the fact that Questfox is a Software as a Service (SaaS) product which has to be accessed by users via a web browser, this solution was excluded from our list of potential evaluation products. For a mutual evaluation of software solutions, it is important to determine a manageable number of evaluation alternatives. By random selection, *MakeItRational, Qualica Decision Suite, SelectPro, easy-mind* and *SuperDecisions* have been determined for our evaluation.

3.2. Evaluation criteria derived from international standard norm

Evaluating software demands to consider commonly understood quality criteria. The first part of the international standard norm ISO/IEC 25010-1:2011 "Systems and software engineering. Systems and software Quality Requirements and Evaluation (SQuaRE). System and software quality models" provides a first foundation for our software evaluation. Scope of this international standard is the definition of a product quality model composed of eight characteristics that relate to static properties of software and dynamic properties of the computer system.

With respect to the evaluation of AHP software products and the underlying standard norm, the focus of interest lies on the product quality from a user's point of view. The quality criteria provided by ISO/IEC are postulated for software evaluations in general. But on account of a certain lack of concreteness with respect to AHP software products, these criteria had to be customized for the teaching and research requirements of the members of the Management Science Department. Thereby, this standard norm is used as a starting point to develop relevant criteria for the evaluation of AHP software products. The results of the transition process are shown in **Figure 1**.

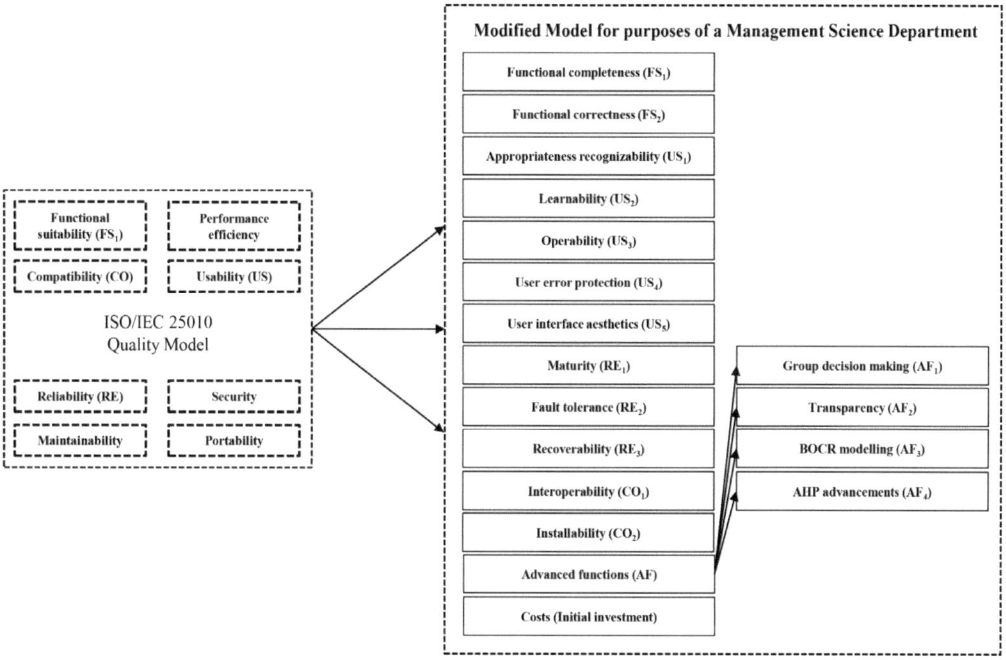

Figure 1. Transition process for criteria identification.

Partial pretests suggested that all software alternatives worked efficiently and secure enough for the department's purposes. Furthermore, there was no need for us to modify the software. Therefore, the criteria performance efficiency, security and maintainability could be disregarded in our model in order to avoid an unnecessarily high level of complexity. Moreover, we added costs and advanced functions as clusters to our model. Within costs, the initial investment was regarded exclusively. The criteria within advanced functions are AHP/ANP-specific as they are derived from special requirements towards Group decision making [19–21], Transparency, Benefits-Opportunities-Costs-Risks (BOCR) modelling [22, 23] and more general AHP advancements. Group decision modelling is an important characteristic as decisions with uncertain attributes often have to be solved in a group context to achieve a broader base of intersubjectivation or objectivity. Furthermore, transparency is necessary for performing sensitivity analysis as well as for the interpretation of the results. In this context, the possibility of BOCR modelling is inevitable for structuring complex strategic decision settings. Apart from structuring, it is moreover possible to cope with scale incommensurability [22, 24–26]. The possibilities of considering horizontal (inter-)dependencies (ANP-extension) or multiplicative AHP [27] are subsumed under AHP advancements.

3.3. DANP-evaluation framework

3.3.1. Application of DANP in literature

As (inter-)dependencies can be assumed between the derived criteria in **Figure 1**, an approach has to be used being able to cope with this kind of criteria structure. So, the ANP moves into focus and is therefore considered to be an adequate evaluation method.

In order to meet our group decision requirements, we additionally use the DEMATEL approach [28–30] for identifying criteria (inter-)dependencies within the ANP evaluation model. Regarding its frequency ranked in the literature [31] shortly beyond fuzzy set theory, DEMATEL belongs to the most common auxiliary tools of ANP—as such denoted by DANP.

In order to highlight the importance of DEMATEL in the field of the ANP literature, we analysed the bibliometric study of Kaspar [15], who used for his study the leading databases EBSCOhost Business Source® Complete, SciVerse® ScienceDirect and Thomson Reuters Web of Knowledge and thus exceeded other bibliometric studies on the ANP [32, 33] to achieve a maximum scope of the literature. The procedure covers three databases and a time horizon from 1998 to 2012 (database accesses for 1998–2011: July 16, 2012 and for 2012: January 28, 2013 [15]). In total, Kaspar found 4187 AHP publications and 613 ANP publications within the databases using the keywords "analytic hierarchy process" and "analytical hierarchy process", respectively, "analytic network process" and "analytical network process" in titles, key words or abstracts [15]. About 52 publications dealt with DEMATEL [15].

Figure 2 [15] gives an overview of AHP and ANP publications from 1998 to 2012. Both methods show a clear upward trend in the timeline, especially rising with the last few years. Although there is a clear growth of ANP related publications, the comparison of total numbers of the publications points out that AHP seems to be more popular in research and practice. This might be due to a lack of software support for ANP and its more complex cognitive requirements. Thereby, evaluating and selecting adequate DSS is an important task to improve the chances of these MCDM methods to be accepted and implemented in a real multi-personal decision contexts. As existing evaluations [16, 18, 34] do not work with advanced approaches as the ANP and/or DEMATEL, and since the 52 publications using DEMATEL within an ANP procedure did not supply any evaluation of AHP software, a new study on this was motivated.

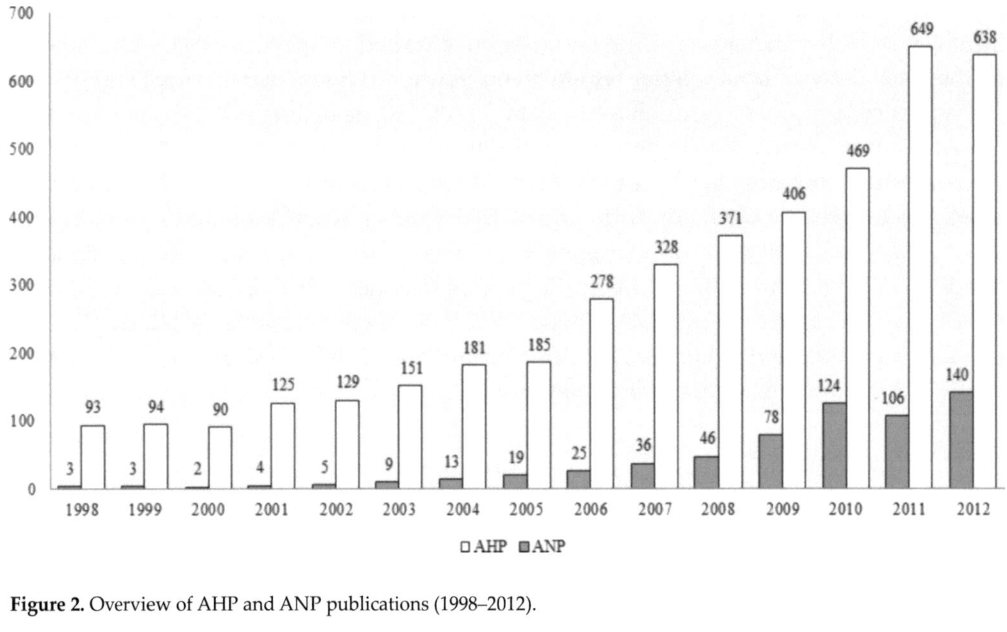

Figure 2. Overview of AHP and ANP publications (1998–2012).

3.3.2. Formal description of DEMATEL for ANP

In order to achieve a better understanding of our evaluation, we start with a short formal explanation of the DEMATEL approach [28]. The initial step within DEMATEL is the determination of the influence values $\propto_{ij}^{r}$ for each decision maker DM_r (r = 1, …, R) for all criteria elements (software alternatives are excluded). The influence values are on an ordinal scale from "0" (no influence) to "4" (extreme strong influence). For synthesizing the group, the next step is to calculate the average matrix $\hat{F}$:

$$\hat{F} = \frac{1}{R} \sum_{r=1}^{R} \left[\propto_{i,j}^{r} \right]_{m \times m}. \tag{1}$$

which has to be normalized by scalar â, in the following way:

$$\hat{F}_{norm} = \frac{\hat{F}}{\hat{a}} \tag{2}$$

$$\hat{a} = \max\left(\max_{1 \leq i \leq m} \sum_{j=1}^{m} \propto_{i,j}, \max_{1 \leq j \leq m} \sum_{i=1}^{m} \propto_{i,j} \right). \tag{3}$$

As a next step, the total-influence matrix $\hat{T}$ is to be calculated as follows in order to consider the indirect effects:

$$\text{where } \lim_{k \to \infty} \hat{F}_{norm}{}^{k} = [\hat{0}]_{m \times m} \tag{4}$$

$$\text{and } \lim_{k \to \infty} \left(\hat{E} + \hat{F}_{norm} + \hat{F}_{norm}{}^{2} + \ldots + \hat{F}_{norm}{}^{k} \right) = \left(\hat{E} - \hat{F}_{norm} \right)^{-1}, \tag{5}$$

$$\text{and } \hat{T} = \hat{E} - \hat{F}_{norm}{}^{k} \text{ or } \hat{T} = \hat{F}_{norm} \left(\hat{E} - \hat{F}_{norm} \right)^{-1}. \tag{6}$$

Having constructed $\hat{T}$, it is necessary to set a threshold value of the required influence level. Only some elements, of which the influence level in matrix F is higher than the threshold value, can be chosen and converted into the impact-digraph-map respectively into the ANP network model [28, 29].

According to the setting of a threshold value, there is no fixed determination rule. It can be decided by experts through discussions [35] or brainstorming [28]. Another possibility would be the exogenous determination by a meta-decision maker. Regardless of the variant of determination, the threshold value should not be too high (too low), as only a few (too many) dependencies would be considered within the ANP model [36].

3.3.3. Construction of the evaluation network model: clustering and dependencies

Before identifying the dependencies within the model, all evaluation criteria have to be assigned to clusters. To cope with scale incommensurability [26], our evaluation model fundamentally consists of the two subnets *Benefits* (with *performance quality* criteria which should be assessed by ordinal judgements) and *Costs* (priorities are derived from monetary values). The overlapping alternatives-cluster consisting of the five AHP-DSS A_1 to A_5 is an integral part of both subnets. The subnet costs contain only one cluster with the element initial investment. The subnet benefits further contains the clusters usability (US), compatibility (CO), functional suitability (FS), reliability (RE) and advanced functions (AF) which are further explained in the evaluation process. All suggested characteristics have to be individually specified to ensure the principle of preferential independence.

Having derived and clustered the relevant criteria and (inter-)dependencies with DEMATEL, the evaluation model is created in a network structure. In order to reach a result representing the different needs of the department's members, the estimations should be the output of a multi-personal estimation, reconsidering different personal requirements with weighed and assessed estimations thus caring for a higher level of intersubjectivity/objectivity. The members of this group—an advanced Master-student (Tutor), academic lecturers and professors—had graduations in Management Science/Business, Informatics and Mathematics, and rated the strength of the dependencies between all model elements within benefits subnet. For assessing the strength of model influences the DEMATEL standard scale with "0 = no interdependency", "1 = low influence", "2 = medium influence", "3 = high influence" and "4 = very high influence" is used. The results in form of $\hat{T}$ are shown in **Table 1** (see the Appendix for individual direct relation matrices $\left[\propto^{r}_{i,j}\right]_{m\times m}$), whereby the number in each cell indicates the influence of the row element on the column element. Following Ou Yang [28] we interpret an influence as essential and considerable if it exceeds a threshold value of 0.1. Such an exceedance characterises an influence as significant and therefore to be subsequently considered in the model of (inter-)dependencies, whereas influences not surpassing this threshold are to be neglected in the model as insignificant. Influences regarded as significant and therefore to be considered are highlighted in the Table by bold numbers. Thereupon the influences are transferred as (inter-)dependencies to the evaluation model to complete the network structure. For improving the overall view of the model, within the ANP approach, the (inter-)dependencies are aggregated by clusters and then visualized by directional arrows. Arrows with double tips are used for representing interdependencies. **Figure 3** shows the final evaluation model for AHP software.

3.4. Assessments and results

3.4.1. Preliminary remarks

Users' individual requirements towards adequate/appropriate software solutions can vary strongly. Therefore, our aim is not primarily to determine a "best DSS" as a general recommendation from the point of view of the members of a Management Science Department. Instead, our evaluation focuses on a transparent confrontation with the 5 heterogeneous products displaying their dependencies and interdependencies within the network of our evaluation criteria.

At an expert workshop, the pairwise comparisons as for the software alternatives' fulfilment of the quality criteria were performed by the authors' mutual agreement to derive a consensus [37]. So, there was no necessity to aggregate the results with the support of a group decision rule. But within a greater department with more experts sharing the evaluation procedure such a rule might have made sense. To evaluate the alternate software products, we constructed a multi-criteria standard problem to be handled by the different DSS. The matrices representing the judgements on Saaty's 1 ("equal importance")-to-9 ("extreme importance") scale [13] are listed below. In the tables, C.R. stands for consistency ratio. The more inconsistent the pairwise judgements, the higher the consistency ratio. Theory suggests that if the consistency ratio for the matrix is not smaller than 0.1, the ratios should be adjusted to make them more consistent. In our evaluation, there was no need for additional adjustments.

http://dx.doi.org/10.5772/67130

	FS_1	FS_2	US_1	US_2	US_3	US_4	US_5	RE_1	RE_2	RE_3	CO_1	CO_2	AF_1	AF_2	AF_3	AF_4
FS_1	0.0276	0.0525	0.0743	**0.1267**	**0.1620**	0.0453	0.0279	0.0600	0.0485	0.0415	0.0830	0.0385	0.0882	**0.1154**	0.0308	**0.1066**
FS_2	0.0130	0.0205	0.0240	0.0990	**0.1013**	0.0456	0.0365	**0.1271**	**0.1128**	0.0304	0.0291	0.0036	0.0100	0.0676	0.0210	0.0126
US_1	0.0014	0.0025	0.0050	0.0347	0.0318	0.0095	0.0118	0.0018	0.0013	0.0003	0.0007	0.0006	0.0019	0.0362	0.0006	0.0015
US_2	0.0025	0.0024	0.0406	0.0203	0.0753	0.0016	0.0383	0.0026	0.0009	0.0004	0.0016	0.0014	0.0026	0.0387	0.0011	0.0022
US_3	0.0200	0.0046	0.0377	**0.1575**	0.0255	0.0031	0.0494	0.0285	0.0049	0.0029	0.0192	0.0182	0.0051	0.0292	0.0027	0.0038
US_4	0.0083	0.0532	0.0104	0.0870	0.0940	0.0095	0.0102	0.0669	0.0884	0.0094	0.0043	0.0025	0.0216	0.0389	0.0028	0.0027
US_5	0.0164	0.0054	0.0741	**0.1602**	**0.1079**	0.0036	0.0129	0.0060	0.0034	0.0014	0.0034	0.0024	0.0290	0.0571	0.0179	0.0203
RE_1	0.0367	0.0806	0.0142	0.0746	**0.1070**	0.0461	0.0196	0.0300	**0.1267**	0.0761	0.0080	0.0116	0.0252	0.0451	0.0203	0.0061
RE_2	0.0340	0.0630	0.0121	0.0769	**0.1080**	0.0511	0.0112	**0.1011**	0.0244	0.0514	0.0145	0.0040	0.0240	0.0350	0.0043	0.0052
RE_3	0.0211	0.0084	0.0056	0.0425	0.0581	0.0219	0.0052	0.0502	0.0501	0.0063	0.0032	0.0021	0.0044	0.0164	0.0018	0.0028
CO_1	0.0246	0.0066	0.0436	0.0347	**0.1020**	0.0047	0.0160	0.0329	0.0230	0.0043	0.0045	0.0194	0.0296	0.0285	0.0187	0.0037
CO_2	0.0228	0.0044	0.0327	0.0262	0.0733	0.0031	0.0058	0.0305	0.0061	0.0033	0.0362	0.0028	0.0205	0.0095	0.0185	0.0027
AF_1	0.0911	0.0315	0.0701	0.0881	**0.1300**	0.0274	0.0305	0.0407	0.0379	0.0162	0.0103	0.0057	0.0136	**0.1131**	0.0052	0.0135
AF_2	0.0179	0.0555	0.0723	**0.1054**	0.0863	0.0299	0.0356	0.0134	0.0114	0.0032	0.0046	0.0022	0.0377	0.0193	0.0107	0.0365
AF_3	0.0808	0.0254	0.0637	0.0738	**0.1023**	0.0075	0.0185	0.0283	0.0256	0.0062	0.0088	0.0047	0.0177	0.0433	0.0038	0.0100
AF_4	0.0908	0.0362	0.0659	0.0847	0.0926	0.0095	0.0195	0.0395	0.0370	0.0080	0.0180	0.0052	0.0278	0.0549	0.0047	0.0114

Table 1. Total influence matrix with final model influences (threshold value = 0.1).

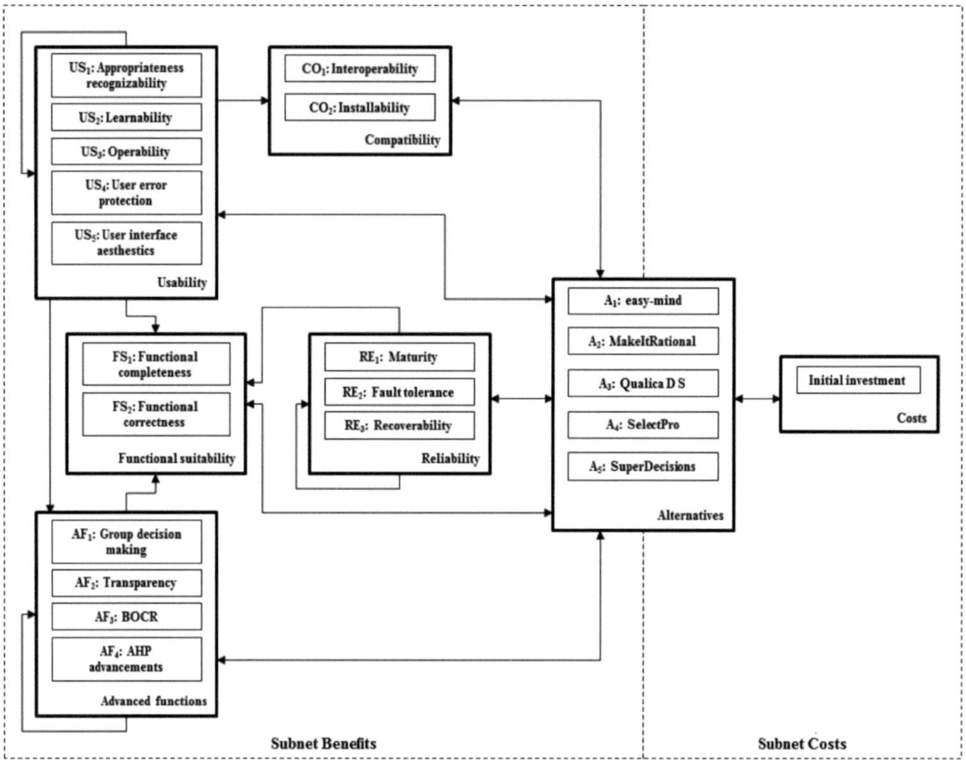

Figure 3. Final DANP-evaluation model for AHP software.

The local priorities of the criteria are shown at the bottom of each table, providing evidence of their importance. The priorities in our study are derived by Saaty's principal eigenvalue method [6, 38, 39].

The next subsection deals with the direct assessments for alternatives' clusters, followed by the presentation of subnets benefits' unweighted supermatrix $\hat{S}^{U}$ and the clustermatrix $\hat{C}$ showing the indirect influences.

3.4.2. Assessments for alternatives cluster

Subsequently, the pairwise comparisons of the DSS alternatives are represented by clusters. Regarding the functional completeness (FS_1, see **Table 2**), all software alternatives except *Qualica Decision Suite*—which cannot handle different alternatives—are equipped with a large and detailed set of functions to handle problems by support of AHP, including dynamic sensitivity analysis, direct data entry and consistency calculation. With respect to the hierarchy to be modelled, the number of criteria, levels and alternatives are not limited in all software products. Highlighting distinctive features, it can be pointed out that *MakeItRational* contains a special alert feature which proposes steps for trouble-shooting when inconsistency reaches 0.1. *SuperDecisions* and *SelectPro* comparatively provide the best sensitivity analysis and the largest set of functions according to direct data entry possibilities. In addition, *SuperDecisions* provides a broader range of rating possibilities (direct priorities, graphically or numbers on 1–9 scale).

Functional suitability	easy-mind	MakeItRational	Qualica D S	SelectPro	SuperDecisions
FS_1: Functional completeness					
C.R. = 0.05793					
easy-mind	1	1/2	7	1/3	1/3
Make ItRational	2	1	8	1/3	1/3
Qualica D S	1/7	1/8	1	1/8	1/9
SelectPro	3	3	8	1	1/2
SuperDecisions	3	3	9	2	1
Local priority	0.11872	0.16196	0.02774	0.29620	0.39538
FS_2: Functional correctness					
C.R. = 0.06412					
easy-mind	1	1/5	7	1/4	1/3
MakeItRational	5	1	9	2	3
Qualica D S	1/7	1/9	1	1/8	1/8
SelectPro	4	1/2	8	1	2
SuperDecisions	3	1/3	8	1/2	1
Local priority	0.09452	0.42264	0.02738	0.27347	0.18199

Table 2. Judgements of the alternatives I (FS).

Within all DSS, the provided functions work correctly (functional correctness, FS_2, see **Table 2**). Due to *Qualica Decision Suite's* inability regarding to the handling of alternatives, it is not possible to achieve a final AHP calculation result. *MakeItRational, SuperDecisions* and *SelectPro* provide a large number of possibilities to show the results either in a graphical way or as data tables. Unfortunately, the given results of *SuperDecisions* and *SelectPro* are sometimes not exact in fourth or fifth decimal place (*SuperDecisions* sometimes curiously displays later on, e.g. 3.0003 instead of the original value of 3.0 inside the evaluation matrices). Furthermore, *MakeItRational* has slight advantages because of its advanced visualization possibilities for the results including alternatives, criteria and ranking comparisons as well as handling of local and global weights.

With respect to the appropriateness [7] of recognizability (US_1, see **Table 3**), *MakeItRational* and *SuperDecisions* provide the best information about the supported functions on their website as well as free trials equipped with the full set of functions, even if *MakeItRational* is slightly more detailed, whereas *SuperDecisions* needs registration to download the trial version. *SelectPro* offers a 30-day and fully functional demo-version without registration, but does not inform about the functions, while *easy-mind's* provided information about the functions is not structured helpfully and partly overhauled. In addition, *easy-mind's* trial is hardly limited in its use of functions. *Qualica Decision Suite* finally allows to download a 30-day trial with all features, but it is absolutely not evident, which functions the software offers or if it supports AHP at all.

Usability	easy-mind	MakeItRational	Qualica D S	SelectPro	SuperDecisions
US_1: Appropriateness recognizability					
C.R. = 0.04383					
easy-mind	1	1/4	7	1/2	1/3
MakeItRational	4	1	9	3	2
Qualica D S	1/7	1/9	1	1/8	1(8
SelectPro	2	1/3	8	1	1/2
SuperDecisions	3	1/2	8	2	1
Local priority	0.11351	0.41896	0.02805	0.17265	0.26683
US_2: Learnability					
C.R. = 0.01875					
easy-mind	1	1/5	3	1/3	3
MakeItRational	5	1	9	3	9
Qualica D S	1/3	1/9	1	1/5	1
SelectPro	3	1/3	5	1	5
SuperDecisions	1/3	1/9	1	1/5	1
Local priority	0.11737	0.53822	0.04817	0.24808	0.04817
US_3: Operability					
C.R. = 0.03498					
easy-mind	1	1/4	4	1/4	4
MakeItRational	4	1	6	1	6
Qualica D S	1/4	1/6	1	1/6	1
SelectPro	4	1	6	1	6
SuperDecisions	1/4	1/6	1	1/6	1
Local priority	0.14386	0.37688	0.05119	0.37688	0.05119
US_4: User error protection					
C.R. = 0.00385					
easy-mind	1	1/3	2	1/2	1
MakeItRational	3	1	5	2	3
Qualica D S	1/2	1/5	1	1/3	1/2
SelectPro	2	1/2	3	1	2
SuperDecisions	1	1/3	2	1/2	1
Local priority	0.13500	0.41428	0.07427	0.24145	0.13500

Usability	easy-mind	MakeItRational	Qualica D S	SelectPro	SuperDecisions
US_5: User interface aesthetics					
C.R. = 0.01131					
easy-mind	1	1/5	1/5	1/8	1/3
MakeItRational	5	1	1	1/2	3
Qualica D S	5	1	1	1/2	3
SelectPro	8	2	2	1	5
SuperDecisions	3	1/3	1/3	1/5	1
Local priority	0.04249	0.22570	0.22570	0.41691	0.08920

Table 3. Judgements of the alternatives II (US).

With regard to the criterion learnability (US_2, see **Table 3**), *MakeItRational, SelectPro* and *easy-mind* are much more intuitively to handle and more advanced in providing assistants, helping hints and tools, online guides and tutorials as well as examples. The other two software alternatives were more difficult to understand with respect to a convenient handling and had a less number of helpful tools.

Operability (US_3, see **Table 3**) was more complex in *Qualica Decision Suite* and *SuperDecisions* and a longer initiation period was needed to operate with these programs. The commands are sometimes hard to find and the next operating step is mostly not obvious. The other three programs are more intuitive in handling, they operate using step-by-step methods. Especially operating with *MakeItRational* and *SelectPro* is easily possible after a very short initiation period.

User error protection (US_4, see **Table 3**) is well-performed in almost all DSS alternatives, the differences are slight. Best hints, handling and protection from errors [7] are implemented in *MakeItRational* and *SelectPro*. Within *MakeItRational*, we did not manage to produce any errors. Owing to the non-step-by-step operating structure of *SuperDecisions*, errors may occur within the working process. *Easy-mind* has to be saved manually by the user after each operating step which produces errors if forgotten.

Regarding the user interface aesthetics (US_5, see **Table 3**), the operation interfaces of *SelectPro, MakeItRational* and *Qualica Decision Suite* are modern, appealing and clearly arranged. In addition, they provide a large set of optical adaptation possibilities according to the needs of the user, for example, the size of the windows, whereby *SelectPro* is notably more professional compared to the other two software alternatives. Although symbols and view are generally clear, the menues and total interface of *easy-mind* are a little amateurish, and it is not possible to make any adaptations. Finally, the menues and structure of *SuperDecisions* are a little too complex and adaptation possibilities are missing, too.

Maturity (RE_1, see **Table 4**) is good in *MakeItRational, Qualica Decision Suite* and *SuperDecisions*. In *SelectPro* occurred some errors using the export functions, while *easy-mind* often produced errors in criteria and alternative management as well as browser errors due to *easy-mind's* nature of a web-based software product.

Reliability	easy-mind	MakeItRational	Qualica D S	SelectPro	SuperDecisions
RE_1: Maturity					
C.R. = 0.00443					
easy-mind	1	1/6	1/6	1/3	1/6
MakeItRational	6	1	1	3	1
Qualica D S	6	1	1	3	1
SelectPro	3	1/3	1/3	1	1/3
SuperDecisions	6	1	1	3	1
Local priority	0.04393	0.28420	0.28420	0.10348	0.28420
RE_2: Fault tolerance					
C.R. = 0.00296					
easy-mind	1	1/4	1/4	1/3	1/4
MakeItRational	4	1	3	3	2
Qualica D S	4	1/3	1	1	1/2
SelectPro	3	1/3	1	1	1/2
SuperDecisions	4	1	1	2	1
Local priority	0.06137	0.26469	0.26469	0.14457	0.26469
RE_3: Recoverability					
C.R. = 0.00000					
easy-mind	1	4	4	4	4
MakeItRational	1/4	1	1	1	1
Qualica D S	1/4	1	1	1	1
SelectPro	1/4	1	1	1	1
SuperDecisions	1/4	1	1	1	1
Local priority	0.50000	0.12500	0.12500	0.12500	0.12500

Table 4. Judgements of the alternatives III (RE).

Regarding *fault tolerance* (RE_2, see **Table 4**), all programs except *easy-mind* were robust and almost operating in a stable manner. Hints on errors and error handling were sometimes missing in *SelectPro*, whereas *easy-mind* was not able to catch most errors which led to a crash of the software.

The recoverability (RE_3, see **Table 4**) of data on error is best solved in *easy-mind* because the user is forced to save each operating step. In all the other software alternatives, data did not get lost if saved before manually by the user.

http://dx.doi.org/10.5772/67130

The interoperability (CO_1, see **Table 5**), especially the export of data, is very strong in *Qualica Decision Suite*, which supports the most important file types. *MakeItRational* and *SelectPro* provide satisfying import and export possibilities (e.g. jpg, doc and xls), although *MakeItRational* is a little more advanced supporting pdf, html and chart images. While *SuperDecisions* is only able to handle MS Excel-importable text files for the super, limit and cluster matrices, *easy-mind* provides no import or export functions at all.

Compatibility	easy-mind	MakeItRational Qualica D S	Qualica D S	SelectPro	SuperDecisions
CO_1: Interoperability					
C.R. = 0.05434					
easy-mind	1	1/8	1/9	1/6	1/2
MakeItRational	8	1	1/3	3	6
Qualica D S	9	3	1	5	8
SelectPro	6	1/3	1/5	1	4
SuperDecisions	2	1/6	1/8	1/4	1
Local priority	0.03251	0.26810	0.51290	0.13744	0.04906
CO_2: Installability					
C.R. = 0.00296					
easy-mind	1	1	3	3	2
MakeItRational	1	1	3	3	2
Qualica D S	1/3	1/3	1	1	1/2
SelectPro	1/3	1/3	1	1	1/2
SuperDecisions	1/2	1/2	2	2	1
Local priority	0.31328	0.31328	0.09857	0.09857	0.17630

Table 5. Judgements of the alternatives IV (CO).

All alternatives run on Windows, which was the testing environment, but installability (CO_2, see **Table 5**) within other systems is not guaranteed for *SelectPro* and *Qualica Decision Suite* by the developer, whereas *SuperDecisions* runs on different versions of Windows, Mac, Ubuntu and Linux. Thereby, *easy-mind* has great advantage due to its nature as independent web-based product as well as *MakeItRational* which can run as desktop version or web-based in a web-browser with MS Silverlight.

Group decision-making (AF_1, see **Table 6**) is implemented in all DSS products except in *SuperDecisions*, but *Qualica Decision Suite* provides only mail questionnaires which have to be inserted by the moderator. The left three software alternatives support remote group decision making, whereby the number of users is only limited in *easy-mind*. *SelectPro* is overall the most professional in rating, calculating the mean and comparing the single user votes.

Advanced functions	easy-mind	MakeItRational	Qualica D S	SelectPro	SuperDecisions
AF_1: Group decision making					
C.R. = 0.04604					
easy-mind	1	1/2	4	1/3	6
MakeItRational	2	1	5	1/2	7
Qualica D S	1/4	1/5	1	1/6	4
SelectPro	3	2	6	1	9
SuperDecisions	1/6	1/7	1/4	1/9	1
Local priority	0.18244	0.27821	0.07216	0.43475	0.03245
AF_2: Transparency					
C.R. = 0.01621					
easy-mind	1	1/4	2	1/6	1
MakeItRational	4	1	5	1/2	5
Qualica D S	1/2	1/5	1	1/7	1/2
SelectPro	6	2	7	1	6
SuperDecisions	1	1/5	2	1/6	1
Local priority	0.08358	0.30371	0.05191	0.48022	0.08058
AF_3: BOCR					
C.R. = 0.00937					
easy-mind	1	3	3	1	1/5
MakeItRational	1/3	1	1	1/3	1/9
Qualica D S	1/3	1	1	1/3	1/9
SelectPro	1	3	3	1	1/5
SuperDecisions	5	9	9	5	1
Local priority	0.14578	0.05389	0.05389	0.14578	0.60066
AF_4: AHP advancements					
C.R. = 0.00000					
easy-mind	1	1	1	1	1/9
MakeItRational	1	1	1	1	1/9
Qualica D S	1	1	1	1	1/9
SelectPro	1	1	1	1	1/9
SuperDecisions	9	9	9	9	1
Local priority	0.07692	0.07692	0.07692	0.07692	0.69231

Table 6. Judgements of the alternatives V (AF).

Transparency (AF_2, see **Table 6**) is strongest in *SelectPro*, which shows at every time and on every level the current results for each user, alternative, criterion, weight and priority as comparable data as well as graphically. Each alternative and criterion can be deselected at each time with automatically actualized results. For the criteria, this is possible in *MakeItRational*, too, which provides slightly less transparency to the user. *SuperDecisions* and *easy-mind* give at least a good overview about the partial results and values of the criteria and alternatives on each level, whereas *Qualica Decision Suite* shows its transparency only regarding the criteria.

Only *SuperDecisions* has implemented a real and good working (pre-structured) Benefits, Opportunities, Costs, Risks (BOCR) modelling (AF_3, see **Table 6**). *SelectPro* supports only cost-score-ratios, while *easy-mind* handles only direct cardinal entries for BOCR. *MakeItRational* and *Qualica Decision Suite* have no implemented BOCR support.

None of the software alternatives except *SuperDecisions* supports any AHP advancements (AF_4, see **Table 6**). However, *SuperDecisions* is the only software product which is able to calculate the results by ANP.

Regarding the costs (initial investment), relevant on account of the financial budget restrictions of the Management Science Department of a medium-sized university, *SuperDecisions* and *easy-mind* were the preferred DSS solutions. Users who understand themselves as researchers or educators can receive both products for free. As there was no ordinal assessment, the local priorities were derived by direct cardinal data entry of the cardinal information (see **Table 7**). Apart from different scaling levels, the criterion initial investment is directed negatively. So, the lowest priorities are assigned to the preferred DSS. This reversed ranking will be transformed in the subsequent synthetization process of the entire model.

Costs					
Initial investment					
C.R. = 0.00000	**easy-mind**	**MakeItRational**	**Qualica D S**	**SelectPro**	**SuperDecisions**
Local priority	0.00060	0.04008	0.90333	0.05539	0.00060

Table 7. Judgements of the alternatives VI (Costs).

Owing to the qualitative expert judgements, all priorities are used now to construct $\hat{S}^U$ (see **Table 8**). Due to the (inter-)dependencies determined by DEMATEL, several cluster comparisons had to be made.

Table 9 shows the arising cluster matrix $\hat{C}$ of the evaluation.

3.4.3. Final results

For deriving the final priorities, as a first step the weighted supermatrix ($\hat{S}^W$) is generated:

$$\hat{S}^W = \hat{S}^U \times \hat{C} \tag{7}$$

Thus, $\hat{S}^{W^k}$ (k = 1, 2, ..., ∞) can be raised, until a converging column-stochastic matrix, the limit matrix ($\hat{S}^L$) is reached.

	FS_1	FS_2	US_1	US_2	US_3	US_4	US_5	RE_1	RE_2	RE_3	CO_1	CO_2	AF_1	AF_2	AF_3	AF_4	A_1	A_2	A_3	A_4	A5
FS_1	0.0000	0.0000	0.0000	1.0000	0.6667	0.0000	0.0000	0.0000	0.0000	0.0000	0.0000	0.0000	0.0000	1.0000	0.0000	1.0000	0.5000	0.5000	0.5000	0.5000	0.5000
FS_2	0.0000	0.0000	0.0000	0.0000	0.3333	0.0000	0.0000	1.0000	1.0000	0.0000	0.0000	0.0000	0.0000	0.0000	0.0000	0.0000	0.5000	0.5000	0.5000	0.5000	0.5000
US_1	0.0000	0.0000	0.0000	0.0000	0.0000	0.0000	0.0000	0.0000	0.0000	0.0000	0.0000	0.0000	0.0000	0.0000	0.0000	0.0000	0.1000	0.1000	0.1000	0.1000	0.1000
US_2	0.0000	0.0000	0.0000	0.0000	0.0000	0.0000	0.0000	0.0000	0.0000	0.0000	0.0000	0.0000	0.0000	0.0000	0.0000	0.0000	0.2500	0.2500	0.2500	0.2500	0.2500
US_3	0.0000	0.0000	0.0000	0.8333	0.0000	0.0000	0.0000	0.0000	0.0000	0.0000	0.0000	0.0000	0.0000	0.0000	0.0000	0.0000	0.2500	0.2500	0.2500	0.2500	0.2500
US_4	0.0000	0.0000	0.0000	0.0000	0.0000	0.0000	0.0000	0.0000	0.0000	0.0000	0.0000	0.0000	0.0000	0.0000	0.0000	0.0000	0.1500	0.1500	0.1500	0.1500	0.1500
US_5	0.0000	0.0000	0.0000	0.1667	1.0000	0.0000	0.0000	0.0000	0.0000	0.0000	0.0000	0.0000	0.0000	0.0000	0.0000	0.0000	0.2500	0.2500	0.2500	0.2500	0.2500
RE_1	0.0000	0.0000	0.0000	0.0000	0.5000	0.0000	0.0000	0.0000	1.0000	0.0000	0.0000	0.0000	0.0000	0.0000	0.0000	0.0000	0.3333	0.3333	0.3333	0.3333	0.3333
RE_2	0.0000	0.0000	0.0000	0.0000	0.5000	0.0000	0.0000	1.0000	0.0000	0.0000	0.0000	0.0000	0.0000	0.0000	0.0000	0.0000	0.3333	0.3333	0.3333	0.3333	0.3333
RE_3	0.0000	0.0000	0.0000	0.0000	0.0000	0.0000	0.0000	0.0000	0.0000	0.0000	0.0000	0.0000	0.0000	0.0000	0.0000	0.0000	0.3333	0.3333	0.3333	0.3333	0.3333
CO_1	0.0000	0.0000	0.0000	0.0000	1.0000	0.0000	0.0000	0.0000	0.0000	0.0000	0.0000	0.0000	0.0000	0.0000	0.0000	0.0000	0.6667	0.6667	0.6667	0.6667	0.6667
CO_2	0.0000	0.0000	0.0000	0.0000	0.0000	0.0000	0.0000	0.0000	0.0000	0.0000	0.0000	0.0000	0.0000	0.0000	0.0000	0.0000	0.3333	0.3333	0.3333	0.3333	0.3333
AF_1	0.0000	0.0000	0.0000	0.0000	0.2000	0.0000	0.0000	0.0000	0.0000	0.0000	0.0000	0.0000	0.0000	1.0000	0.0000	0.0000	0.2000	0.2000	0.2000	0.2000	0.2000
AF_2	0.0000	0.0000	0.0000	1.0000	0.0000	0.0000	0.0000	0.0000	0.0000	0.0000	0.0000	0.0000	0.0000	0.0000	0.0000	0.0000	0.2000	0.2000	0.2000	0.2000	0.2000
AF_3	0.0000	0.0000	0.0000	0.0000	0.8000	0.0000	0.0000	0.0000	0.0000	0.0000	0.0000	0.0000	0.0000	0.0000	0.0000	0.0000	0.4000	0.4000	0.4000	0.4000	0.4000
AF_4	0.0000	0.0000	0.0000	0.0000	0.0000	0.0000	0.0000	0.0000	0.0000	0.0000	0.0000	0.0000	0.0000	0.0000	0.0000	0.0000	0.2000	0.2000	0.2000	0.2000	0.2000
A_1	0.1187	0.0945	0.1135	0.1174	0.1439	0.1350	0.0425	0.0439	0.0614	0.5000	0.0325	0.3133	0.1824	0.0836	0.1458	0.0769	0.0000	0.0000	0.0000	0.0000	0.0000
A_2	0.1620	0.4226	0.4190	0.5382	0.3769	0.4143	0.2257	0.2842	0.2647	0.1250	0.2681	0.3133	0.2782	0.3037	0.0539	0.0769	0.0000	0.0000	0.0000	0.0000	0.0000
A_3	0.0277	0.0274	0.0280	0.0482	0.0512	0.0743	0.2257	0.2842	0.2647	0.1250	0.5129	0.0986	0.0722	0.0519	0.0539	0.0769	0.0000	0.0000	0.0000	0.0000	0.0000
A_4	0.2962	0.2735	0.1726	0.2481	0.3769	0.2414	0.4169	0.1035	0.1446	0.1250	0.1374	0.0986	0.4347	0.4802	0.1458	0.0769	0.0000	0.0000	0.0000	0.0000	0.0000
A_5	0.3954	0.1820	0.2668	0.0482	0.0512	0.1350	0.0892	0.2842	0.2647	0.1250	0.0491	0.1763	0.0325	0.0806	0.6007	0.6923	0.0000	0.0000	0.0000	0.0000	0.0000

Table 8. Unweighted supermatrix $\hat{S}^{u}$ subnet benefits.

	Functional suitability (FS)	Usability (US)	Reliability (RE)	Compatibility (CO)	Advanced Functions (AF)	Alternatives (A)
Functional suitability (FS)	0.0000	0.1667	0.5190	0.0000	0.3333	0.0000
Usability (US)	0.0000	0.1667	0.0000	0.0000	0.0000	0.0000
Reliability (RE)	0.0000	0.1667	0.1775	0.0000	0.0000	0.0000
Compatibility (CO)	0.0000	0.1667	0.0000	0.0000	0.0000	0.0000
Advanced functions (AF)	0.0000	0.1667	0.0000	0.0000	0.3333	0.0000
Alternatives (A)	0.0000	0.1667	0.3035	1.0000	0.3333	0.0000

Table 9. Cluster matrix ($\hat{C}$) subnet benefits.

The final synthesized (additive probabilistic variant) ranking of the software products is shown in **Figure 4**. Thereby, the overall control criteria weighting for subnet benefits was set to 0.8 and to 0.2 for subnet costs (preferential value 4 on standard scale).

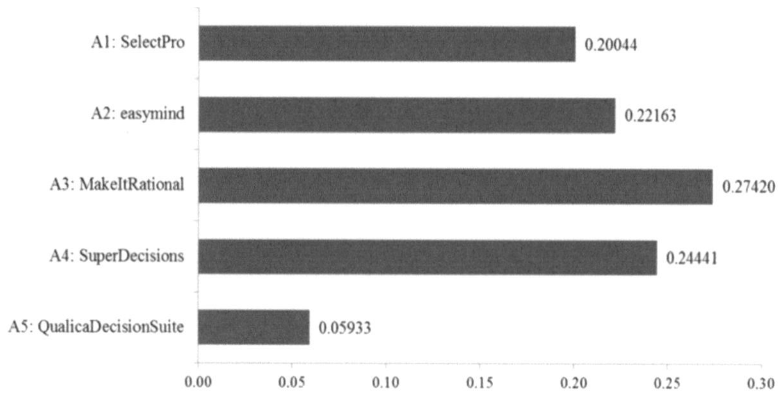

Figure 4. Synthesized evaluation results (global priorities of the software products).

Owing to our subjective judgements, *MakeItRational* was found to be the preferred software alternative for the purposes of an academic Management Science Department, followed by *SuperDecisions, easy-mind* and *SelectPro*. The results show that there is a small distance regarding the level of performance. Regarding the other quality criteria, the differences between these programs are not extreme, but noticeable. Therefore, different rankings could result, if members of other academic departments or of other types of organizations with deviating targets, requirements, preferences and size would have evaluated the alternative software solutions. So, there may exist contexts, in which another software product than *MakeItRational* would fit better to the needs of the users.

MakeItRational, easy-mind and *SelectPro*, e.g. are convincing due to their very intuitive handling and step-by-step operating methods. The commands are obvious to find and easy to understand, mostly supported by helping functions or assistants. In general, the initiation period to operate with these programs is very short. Among all software products, *MakeItRational* is the most intuitive and the less complex. Besides, it provides more visualization and export possibilities and has the best error protection.

But especially when BOCR modelling or ANP is needed within the decision process, *SuperDecisions* is the only alternative within which these functions are implemented. Additionally, it offers more possibilities and functions than *MakeItRational* that go beyond the pure AHP application. But, this charges at learnability and operability. Furthermore, this product provides no group decision-making support, which is handled best and most detailed by *SelectPro,* being in this respect a good alternative to MakeItRational. It is the most professional in rating, calculating the mean and comparing the single votes. Besides, it scores by its transparency, showing current results at every time and on every level as comparable data as well as graphically.

4. ANP-based evaluation assisted by parallel and distributed computing

The described procedure comprised the structuring of software quality criteria and an evaluation of alternative AHP-supporting software products in the multi-personnel framework of a Management Science Department of a medium-sized university. This proceeding delivers an object of reference to solve such structuring and evaluation problems in a modified situation by assistance of parallel and/or distributed computing architecture [7]. If the number of experts, whose requirements towards alternative software products diverge, essentially enhances (compared with the state of affairs in the aforementioned department) and/or if the complexity of the network structure relevant for the evaluation increases considerably, such a computing architecture would be advantageous.

Problems to be solved on a strategic decision level with a demand for scientific computing might attain a degree of complexity that distributed computing architectures are to be recommended. The more complex the ANP-network structure, the more the modelled problem delivers connecting factors for such architectures. With its possibilities to intensify the "interaction" among different criteria [7, 40], their interlacing can be represented within and between the ANP-clusters more clearly. Thus, distributed computing would help to cope with increasing complexity of multi-criteria-decision relevant network structures.

The higher the number of experts and the variety of their requirements for software quality, the more advantageous would be a parallel computing [7] which enables faster computational results [40]. Such computing architectures can support learning processes among the members of an expert group which evaluate the quality of alternative software products simultaneously within the framework of a multi-personnel, interactive process.

5. Conclusion

MCDM-DSS is an important tool aid for solving complex strategic decision problems as, e.g. arising in a Management Science Department of a medium-sized university. Such a support has to suffice the heterogeneous teaching and research tasks of different persons in different functions with deviating experiences, requirements and preferences. For these tasks and the inhered strategic decisions, AHP and ANP are suitable decision support methods. Problems on a standard level of complexity should be solved by AHP, whereby an increasing connectivity induces the application of ANP. Both approaches are subject to a growing importance. At this time, AHP is relatively more important than ANP in the literature due to less sophisticated mathematical calculations but also to a longer existence of the method. A vast number of strategic decision problems can be handled with AHP. Therefore, an adequate DSS is necessary for ensuring mathematical correct method application as well as to bring forward the application of this method.

Owing to the great variety of AHP-DSS, the aim of this paper was a transparent evaluation of five heterogeneous products from the point of view of the members of a Management Science Department. In this context, it was not the aim to give a generalized recommendation for one of these products, but to highlight the distinctive differences and special features of the evaluated products. Thereby, criteria have been derived from ISO/IEC norm and used. As the evaluation was considered as a problem with a higher complexity (connectivity), the ANP was used. In order to integrate the specifically inclined states of knowledge of different department members and to ensure a higher degree of inter-subjectivity, five members of the academic staff with different teaching and research experiences and functions estimated (inter-)dependencies between criteria of software quality. Then, a rating of randomly selected software products as for the fulfilment of the quality criteria took place. To improve the ANP modelling regarding the identification of (inter-)dependencies as well as to meet the requirements of the group members, DEMATEL as the second most important ANP auxiliary tool was added to the evaluation framework. With a combination of DEMATEL and ANP (DANP), a solid framework for the multi-personnel evaluation has been established. Against the backdrop of a certain need of AHP-DSS and a certain lack of adequate software evaluations, the application of DANP to supply the need was pointed out.

It has become clear that the development of further ANP-DSS products can be advised, as well as an integration of DEMATEL into the DSS of AHP and ANP. Furthermore, there is a need for case studies in the field of DEMATEL combined with AHP and ANP which can further clarify and highlight the potential of such a combination and facilitate its usage in practice. The more experts with diverging software quality requirements are sharing the structuring and evaluating process, the more advantageous it would be to assist the procedure by parallel computing architectures. And with increasing complexity of the quality criteria's network, the development of such a structure by an expert group will be more efficient if supported by distributed computing architectures.

Acknowledgments

Dr. Stefanie Schinke and Dipl.-Kfm. Fabian Burrey, M.Sc., are thanked for their participation in the group evaluation procedure.

Appendix 1

DM_1	FS_1	FS_2	US_1	US_2	US_3	US_4	US_5	RE_1	RE_2	RE_3	CO_1	CO_2	AF_1	AF_2	AF_3	AF_4
FS_1	0	1	1	2	2	0	0	1	0	0	1	0	0	2	0	3
FS_2	0	0	1	0	0	0	0	0	0	0	0	0	0	0	0	0
US_1	0	0	0	0	0	0	0	0	0	0	0	0	0	0	0	0
US_2	0	0	2	0	0	0	0	0	0	0	0	0	0	0	0	0
US_3	0	0	0	4	0	0	1	0	0	0	0	0	0	0	0	0
US_4	0	4	0	1	3	0	0	3	3	0	0	0	0	0	0	0
US_5	0	0	2	2	2	0	0	0	0	0	0	0	0	0	0	0
RE_1	0	0	0	0	3	0	0	0	3	0	0	0	0	0	0	0
RE_2	0	0	0	0	3	0	0	1	0	3	0	0	0	0	0	0
RE_3	0	0	0	0	1	0	0	0	0	0	0	0	0	0	0	0
CO_1	0	0	1	0	2	0	0	0	0	0	0	2	0	0	0	0
CO_2	0	0	0	0	0	0	0	0	0	0	2	0	0	0	0	0
AF_1	0	0	3	2	2	0	0	1	1	1	0	0	0	2	0	0
AF_2	0	2	3	2	2	0	0	0	0	0	0	0	2	0	0	0
AF_3	0	0	3	2	2	0	0	0	0	0	0	0	0	0	0	0
AF_4	0	0	3	2	2	0	0	0	0	0	0	0	0	0	0	0

Appendix 2

DM_1	FS_1	FS_2	US_1	US_2	US_3	US_4	US_5	RE_1	RE_2	RE_3	CO_1	CO_2	AF_1	AF_2	AF_3	AF_4
FS_1	0	0	0	0	3	0	0	0	0	0	1	0	2	1	0	1
FS_2	0	0	0	4	4	2	0	3	2	0	3	0	0	0	0	0
US_1	0	0	0	0	0	0	0	0	0	0	0	0	0	0	0	0
US_2	0	0	0	0	0	0	0	0	0	0	0	0	0	1	0	0

DM_1	FS_1	FS_2	US_1	US_2	US_3	US_4	US_5	RE_1	RE_2	RE_3	CO_1	CO_2	AF_1	AF_2	AF_3	AF_4
US_3	0	0	0	2	0	0	0	3	0	0	2	2	0	0	0	0
US_4	0	0	0	0	0	0	0	3	2	0	0	0	0	0	0	0
US_5	0	0	0	4	0	0	0	0	0	0	0	0	0	0	0	0
RE_1	0	0	0	0	0	0	0	0	3	3	0	0	0	0	0	0
RE_2	0	0	0	0	0	1	0	1	0	0	0	0	0	0	0	0
RE_3	0	0	0	0	0	0	0	2	0	0	0	0	0	0	0	0
CO_1	0	0	0	0	3	0	0	0	0	0	0	0	0	0	0	0
CO_2	0	0	0	0	2	0	0	2	0	0	0	0	0	0	0	0
AF_1	4	0	0	0	4	0	0	0	0	0	0	0	0	4	0	0
AF_2	0	2	0	2	0	0	0	0	0	0	0	0	0	0	1	4
AF_3	4	0	0	0	4	0	0	0	0	0	0	0	0	0	0	0
AF_4	4	0	0	0	0	0	0	0	0	0	0	0	0	0	0	0

Appendix 3

DM_1	FS_1	FS_2	US_1	US_2	US_3	US_4	US_5	RE_1	RE_2	RE_3	CO_1	CO_2	AF_1	AF_2	AF_3	AF_4
FS_1	0	1	3	4	4	3	1	2	2	4	4	4	3	4	3	4
FS_2	0	0	0	2	2	0	3	4	4	0	0	0	0	4	1	0
US_1	0	0	0	2	2	1	0	0	0	0	0	0	0	4	0	0
US_2	0	0	1	0	4	0	1	0	0	0	0	0	0	1	0	0
US_3	2	0	2	4	0	0	0	0	0	0	0	0	0	0	0	0
US_4	0	0	0	4	4	0	0	0	2	0	0	0	2	3	0	0
US_5	1	0	2	4	4	0	0	0	0	0	0	0	3	4	2	2
RE_1	3	4	0	3	4	4	1	0	4	2	0	0	2	3	2	0
RE_2	3	4	0	3	4	3	0	4	0	2	1	0	2	2	0	0
RE_3	2	0	0	1	3	0	0	0	0	0	0	0	0	1	0	0
CO_1	2	0	3	1	3	0	1	2	2	0	0	0	3	2	2	0
CO_2	2	0	3	1	3	0	0	1	0	0	2	0	2	0	2	0
AF_1	2	2	3	3	3	2	2	2	2	0	0	0	0	3	0	0
AF_2	1	0	4	4	4	3	3	0	0	0	0	0	2	0	0	0
AF_3	2	2	3	3	3	0	1	2	2	0	0	0	1	3	0	0
AF_4	4	3	3	4	4	0	1	3	3	0	1	0	2	4	0	0

Appendix 4

DM_1	FS_1	FS_2	US_1	US_2	US_3	US_4	US_5	RE_1	RE_2	RE_3	CO_1	CO_2	AF_1	AF_2	AF_3	AF_4
FS_1	0	0	1	2	2	0	0	0	0	0	3	0	4	3	0	2
FS_2	0	0	0	0	0	1	0	4	4	0	0	0	0	2	0	0
US_1	0	0	0	1	1	0	1	0	0	0	0	0	0	0	0	0
US_2	0	0	1	0	4	0	3	0	0	0	0	0	0	2	0	0
US_3	0	0	1	4	0	0	4	0	0	0	0	0	0	2	0	0
US_4	0	0	0	0	0	0	0	0	2	0	0	0	0	0	0	0
US_5	0	0	3	4	4	0	0	0	0	0	0	0	0	1	0	0
RE_1	0	0	0	0	0	0	0	0	3	3	0	0	0	0	0	0
RE_2	0	0	0	1	2	1	0	1	0	0	0	0	0	0	0	0
RE_3	0	0	0	1	1	2	0	3	3	0	0	0	0	0	0	0
CO_1	0	0	0	0	2	0	0	0	0	0	0	0	0	0	0	0
CO_2	0	0	0	0	2	0	0	0	0	0	0	0	0	0	0	0
AF_1	3	0	0	0	2	0	0	0	0	0	0	0	0	2	0	0
AF_2	0	2	0	0	1	0	0	0	0	0	0	0	0	0	0	0
AF_3	2	0	0	0	0	0	0	0	0	0	0	0	0	0	0	0
AF_4	2	0	0	0	1	0	0	0	0	0	0	0	0	0	0	0

Appendix 5

DM_1	FS_1	FS_2	US_1	US_2	US_3	US_4	US_5	RE_1	RE_2	RE_3	CO_1	CO_2	AF_1	AF_2	AF_3	AF_4
FS_1	0	2	0	0	1	1	0	1	1	0	0	0	0	0	0	2
FS_2	0	0	0	1	1	1	0	2	1	2	0	0	0	0	1	1
US_1	0	0	0	0	0	0	0	0	0	0	0	0	0	0	0	0
US_2	0	0	0	0	0	0	0	0	0	0	0	0	0	0	0	0
US_3	0	0	0	3	0	0	0	0	0	0	0	0	0	0	0	0
US_4	0	1	0	2	1	0	0	0	0	0	0	0	0	0	0	0
US_5	0	0	0	2	0	0	0	0	0	0	0	0	0	0	0	0
RE_1	0	4	0	1	1	0	0	0	0	0	0	1	0	0	0	0
RE_2	0	2	0	1	0	0	0	3	0	0	0	0	0	0	0	0
RE_3	0	0	0	1	0	0	0	0	2	0	0	0	0	0	0	0
CO_1	0	0	0	0	0	0	0	1	0	0	0	0	0	0	0	0

DM_1	FS_1	FS_2	US_1	US_2	US_3	US_4	US_5	RE_1	RE_2	RE_3	CO_1	CO_2	AF_1	AF_2	AF_3	AF_4
CO_2	0	0	0	0	0	0	0	0	0	0	0	0	0	0	0	0
AF_1	**1**	0	0	0	**0**	0	0	0	0	0	0	0	0	**0**	0	0
AF_2	0	0	0	**1**	0	0	0	0	0	0	0	0	0	0	0	0
AF_3	**1**	0	0	0	**0**	0	0	0	0	0	0	0	0	0	0	0
AF_4	0	0	0	0	0	0	0	0	0	0	0	0	0	0	0	0

Author details

Wolfgang Ossadnik*, Ralf H. Kaspar and Benjamin Föcke

*Address all correspondence to: wolfgang.ossadnik@uos.de

Department of Management Science/Management Accounting and Control, University of Osnabrück, Osnabrück, Germany

References

[1] Pearce J A I, Robinson R B. Formulation and Implementation of Competitive Strategy. 3rd ed. Homewood, IL: Irwin; 1988. 447 p.

[2] Charnes A, Cooper W W, Ferguson R O. Optimal estimation of executive compensation by linear programming. Management Science. 1955;**1**(2):138-151. doi:10.1287/mnsc.1.2.138

[3] Charnes A, Cooper W W. Management Models and Industrial Applications of Linear Programming. 1st ed. New York: John Wiley; 1961. 467 p.

[4] Charnes A, Cooper W W. Goal programming and multiple objective optimizations: Part 1. European Journal of Operational Research. 1977;**1**(1):39-54. doi:10.1016/S0377-2217(77)81007-2

[5] Hülle J, Kaspar R, Möller K. Multiple criteria decision-making in management accounting and control—state of the art and research perspectives based on a bibliometric study. Journal of Multi-Criteria Decision Analysis. 2011;**18**(5-6):253-265. doi:10.1002/mcda.482

[6] Saaty T L. The Analytical Hierarchy Process. 1st ed. New York: McGraw-Hill; 1980. 287 p.

[7] Hwang K, Dongarra J J, Fox G C. Distributed and Cloud Computing. From Parallel Processing to the Internet of Things. 1st ed. Amsterdam: Morgan Kaufmann; 2011. 672 p.

[8] Saaty T L. Axiomatic foundation of the analytic hierarchy process. Management Science. 1986;**32**(7):841-855. doi:10.1287/mnsc.32.7.841

[9] Saaty T L, Vargas L G. Models, Methods, Concepts & Applications of the Analytic Hierarchy Process. 1st ed. Boston: Kluwer Academic Publishers; 2001. 333 p. doi:10.1007/978-1-4615-1665-1

[10] Saaty T L. Decision Making with Dependence and Feedback: The Analytic Network Process. 1st ed. Pittsburgh: RWS Publications; 1996.

[11] Saaty T L. Decision Making with Dependence and Feedback: The Analytical Network Process. 2nd ed. Pittsburgh: RWS Publications; 2001. 370 p.

[12] Saaty T L. Making and validating complex decisions with the AHP/ANP. Journal of Systems Science and Systems Engineering. 2005;**14**(1):1-36. doi:10.1007/s11518-006-0179-6

[13] Saaty T L, Vargas L G. Decision Making With the Analytic Network Process. 2nd ed. New York: Springer; 2013. 363 p. doi:10.1007/978-1-4614-7279-7

[14] Saaty T L. Decision Making in Complex Environments—The Analytic Hierarchy Process (AHP) and The Analytic Network Process (ANP) for Decision Making with Dependence and Feedback (SuperDecisions Tutorial) [Internet]. 2003. Available from: www.superdecisions.com [Accessed: 10/31/2016].

[15] Kaspar R. Holistic Analysis and Evaluation of strategy options [Ganzheitliche Analyse und Bewertung von Strategie-Optionen]. 1st ed. Göttingen: Cuvillier; 2014. 420 p.

[16] Ossadnik W, Lange O. AHP-based evaluation of AHP-Software. European Journal of Operational Research. 1999;**118**(3):578-588. doi:10.1016/S0377-2217(98)00321-X

[17] Ishizaka A, Nemery P. Multi-criteria Decision Analysis—Methods and Software. 1st ed. Chichester: Wiley; 2013. 310 p.

[18] Ossadnik W, Kaspar R. Evaluation of AHP software from a management accounting perspective. Journal of Modelling in Management. 2013;**8**(3):305-319. doi:10.1108/JM2-01-2011-0007

[19] Dyer R F, Forman E H. Group decision support with the Analytic Hierarchy Process. Decision Support Systems. 1992;**8**(2):99-124. doi:10.1016/0167-9236(92)90003-8

[20] Forman E H, Peniwati K. Aggregating individual judgments and priorities with the Analytic Hierarchy Process. European Journal of Operational Research. 1996;**108**(1):165-169. doi:10.1016/S0377-2217(97)00244-0

[21] Altuzarra A, Moreno-Jiménez J M, Salvador M. A Bayesian priorization procedure for AHP-group decision making. European Journal of Operational Research. 2007;**182**(1):367-382. doi:10.1016/j.ejor.2006.07.025

[22] Wijnmalen D J D. Analysis of benefits, opportunities, costs, and risks (BOCR) with the AHP–ANP: a critical validation. Mathematical and Computer Modelling. 2007;**46**(7-8):892-905. doi:10.1016/j.mcm.2007.03.020

[23] Azizi M, Azizipour M. A BOCR structure for privatisation effective criteria of Iran newsprint paper industry. International Journal of Production Research. 2012;**50**(17):4867-4876. doi:10.1080/00207543.2012.657973

[24] Choo E U, Schoner B, Wedley W C. Interpretation of criteria weights in multicriteria decision making. Computers & Industrial Engineering. 1999;**37**(3):527-541. doi:10.1016/S0360-8352(00)00019-X

[25] Wedley W C, Choo E U, Schoner B. Magnitude adjustment for AHP benefit/cost ratio. European Journal of Operational Research. 2001;**133**(2):342-351. doi:10.1016/S0377-2217(00)00302-7

[26] Wedley W C, Choo E U, Wijnmalen D J D. Benefit/Cost Priorities—Achieving Commensurability. In: Proceedings of the Annual Conference of the Administrative Sciences Association of Canada—ASAC 2003; June 14-17 2003; Halifax Nova Scotia. Halifax Nova Scotia: Management Science Division; 2003. pp. 85-94.

[27] Triantaphyllou E. Two new cases of rank reversals when the AHP and some of its additive variants are used that do not occur with the multiplicative AHP. Journal of Multi-Criteria Decision Analysis. 2001;**10**(1):11-25. doi:10.1002/mcda.284

[28] Ou Yang Y P, Shieh H M, Leu J D, Tzeng G. A novel hybrid MCDM model combined with DEMATEL and ANP with applications. International Journal of Operations Research. 2008;**5**(3):160-168.

[29] Yang J L, Tzeng G. An Integrated MCDM technique combined with DEMATEL for a novel cluster-weighted with ANP method. Expert Systems with Applications. 2011;**38**(3):1417-1424. doi:10.1016/j.eswa.2010.07.048

[30] Sumrit D, Anuntavoranich P. Using DEMATEL method to analyze the causal relations on technological innovation capability evaluation factors in thai technology-based firms. International Transaction Journal of Engineering, Management, & Applied Sciences & Technologies. 2013;**4**(2):81-103.

[31] Liou J H. New concepts and trends of MCDM for tomorrow. Technological & Economic Development of Economy. 2013;**19**(2):367-375. doi:10.3846/20294913.2013.811037

[32] Vaidya O S, Kumar S. Analytic hierarchy process: an overview of applications. European Journal of Operational Research. 2006;**169**(1):1-29. doi:10.1016/j.ejor.2004.04.028

[33] Sipahi S, Timor M. The analytic hierarchy process and analytic network process: an overview of application. Management Decision. 2010;**48**(5):775-808. doi:10.1108/00251741011043920

[34] Ishizaka A, Labib A. Analytic Hierarchy Process and Expert Choice: Benefits and Limitations. ORInsight. 2009;**22**(4):201-220. doi:10.1057/ori.2009.10

[35] Tzeng G, Chen W H, Shih M L. Fuzzy decision maps: a generalization of the DEMATEL methods. Soft Computing. 2010;**14**(11):1141-1150. doi:10.1007/s00500-009-0507-0

[36] Tsai W H, Hsu W. A novel hybrid model based on DEMATEL and ANP for selecting cost of quality model development. Total Quality Management. 2010;**21**(4):439-456. doi:10.1080/14783361003606852

[37] Saaty T L. Group Decision Making and the AHP. In: Golden B L, Wasil E A, Harker P T, editors. The Analytical Hierarchy Process. 1st ed. Berlin: Springer; 1989. pp. 59-67. doi:10.1007/978-3-642-50244-6_4

[38] Saaty T L. A scaling method for priorities in hierarchical structures. Journal of Mathematical Psychology. 1977;**15**(3):234-281. doi:10.1016/0022-2496(77)90033-5

[39] Ishizaka A, Lusti M. How to derive priorities in AHP: a comparative study. Central European Journal of Operations Research. 2006;**14**(4):387-400. doi:10.1007/s10100-006-0012-9

[40] Erciyes, K. Distributed and Sequential Algorithms for Bioinformatics. Computational Biology, 23, 1st ed. New York: Springer; 2015. 367 p.